Leigh Girls' Grammar School Swift and Sure

Julie McKiernan

For Avis Freeman, who has kept the flame of LGGS burning,
and all the wonderful women who made it a school to remember.

Author's Note

Julie McKiernan lives in Leigh, Greater Manchester. At Leigh Girls' Grammar School (LGGS), and then Westleigh High School, she wrote short plays to be performed in assemblies and was a keen member of the school drama group. She did her A-Levels at Leigh College, and returned there several years later, with a degree, to teach Performing Arts and Creative Writing. After twenty-five years, she was made redundant, had bowel surgery for Crohn's Disease, and became a full-time freelance writer. Specialising in heritage writing, she has written personal life stories, local history essays, the histories of local companies and organisations, guided heritage trails and scripts about people, places and events. She has had plays performed and work-shopped by professional theatre companies, and she has written and directed two plays performed by Leigh Centurions rugby league players.

This book is a labour of love.

Table of Contents

ILLUSTRATIONS

Every effort has been made to trace the copyright holders and obtain permission to reproduce this material. Please do get in touch with any enquiries or any information relating to these images or the rights holder.

Sources of images

1. LGGS from church (Susan Duckworth collection)
2. 1921 Opening Ceremony of LGGS (Archives: Wigan & Leigh)
3. Miss Caress (LGGS magazine/Archives: Wigan & Leigh)
4. Miss Perrott (LGGS magazine/Archives: Wigan & Leigh)
5. Miss Nanney (LGGS magazine/Archives: Wigan & Leigh)
6. Miss Shanks (Park School Collection)
7. Miss Hulme (LGGS magazine/Archives: Wigan & Leigh)
8. Miss Swindells (LGGS magazine/Archives: Wigan & Leigh)
9. Miss Smart (LGGS magazine/Archives: Wigan & Leigh)
10. The Head Girls board (Caroline Ellison collection)
11. Pre-1921 at RR(Archives: Wigan & Leigh)
12. Pre-1921 at Railway Road Hockey (Archives: Wigan & Leigh)
13. Miss Gregory, Latin (Avis Freeman collection)
14. Miss Osgood, English (Avis Freeman collection)
15. Miss Wood PT (Avis Freeman collection)
16. 1930s LGGS tunic (Avis Freeman collection)
17. 1934 Paris Holiday (Avis Freeman collection)
18. 1936 Pennygrove Holiday (Avis Freeman collection)

19. 1936 Pennygrove uniform (Avis Freeman collection)
20. 1936 Tree Planting (Avis Freeman collection)
21. 1949 staff (Avis Freeman collection)
22. 1940s (Steve Crook collection)
23. Whiteacre Camp 1949 (Avis Freeman collection)
24. 1948-9 Netball Team (LGGS magazine/Archives: Wigan & Leigh)
25. 1940s Head Girl badge (Brenda Armitage collection)
26. 1958 Paris (Avis Freeman collection)
27. 1950s Sketching in the churchyard (John Sumner collection)
28. 1951Taming of the Shrew (LGGS magazine/Archives: Wigan & Leigh)
29. 1950s School pitch (Vivien J. Davies collection)
30. 1950s trip in snow (Vivien J. Davies collection)
31. 1960s School Field (Avis Freeman collection)
32. 1961 OGA (Avis Freeman collection)
33. 1960s Staff at field (Avis Freeman collection)
34. 1960s Uniform (Sheila Crawley collection)
35. 1960s School dress (Julie McKiernan collection/Gail Lloyd)
36. 1975 Miss Smart & Miss Wooley (Anne Eccleshare collection)
37. 1973 Chester Zoo (Avis Freeman collection)
38. 1973 Mr Williams in drag (Avis Freeman collection)
39. 1973 Staff entertainment (Avis Freeman collection)
40. 1975 Timetable IV year (Yvonne Parr collection)
41. Ground Floor Plan (Julie McKiernan collection)
42. 1930s Gym (Archives: Wigan & Leigh)
43. 1930s School Hall (Archives: Wigan & Leigh)
44. 1930s Geography (Archives: Wigan & Leigh)
45. Upper Floor Plan (Julie McKiernan collection)
46. 1930s Domestic Science (Archives: Wigan & Leigh)
47. 1930s Chemistry (Archives: Wigan & Leigh)
48. 1930s Library (Archives: Wigan & Leigh)

The Homework

In 1994, Avis Freeman, ex-LGGS pupil and teacher, decided there should be a book about Leigh Girls' Grammar School (LGGS) and asked old girls to send her their memories. Quite a few responded but, despite her enthusiasm, Avis could never find the time or energy to write the book. She did, however, keep all the letters and would ask at the Old Girls' Reunion Dinner each year for further memories and information. Almost twenty-five years later, Teresa May proposed grammar schools should be reintroduced and I realised that the pupils at Bedford High School, based in the former boys-only Leigh Grammar School (LGS) building on Manchester Road, Leigh, would not understand what this meant. At the same time, it became clear to us that the youngest ex-LGGS girls and LGS boys would now be in their fifties. Unless we acted quickly, we would lose the opportunity to capture the memories of both sets of staff and students. So, as Healthy Arts, a not-for-profit arts and heritage organisation, we applied to the Heritage Lottery Young Roots programme to fund a 'Leigh Grammar Schools Heritage Project'.

We were successful and, working in partnership with young people from Bedford High School and with Archives: Wigan & Leigh, we spent nine months meeting old girls and boys and former staff, collecting their memories and artefacts. It was amazing what re-emerged after years hidden away in cupboards, boxes and lofts: from items of uniform, badges and certificates, to text books, exam papers and even acceptance letters. We ended the project, in July 2018, with a wonderful Celebration Day at Bedford High which included a large exhibition, an opportunity to answer 11+ exam questions, dramatic performances about life at both schools, and a debate about grammar school education (more information on this event can be found at http://www.healthyarts.org.uk/past-leigh-grammar.html).

Everything we collected during the project from recorded group and individual interviews, letters and social media posts, was donated to the Archives, and Avis finally found a safe place to store her huge personal collection of memorabilia.

But there still wasn't a book. So I decided I would write one. In early 2019 I started to research the history of LGGS by working my way through the Leigh Town Council minutes. I found enough information to create the opening chapter, then life got in the way and it wasn't until the first Lockdown of 2020 that I decided to revisit my notes and make good use of my time. When Avis pointed out that 2021 would be the centenary of the school, I had my deadline. And so I began.

Over the course of the next year I worked my way through all of the letters that had been sent to Avis, determined that those lovely ladies, most of them no longer with us, would have their place in history. The next question was how to decide on the structure, what to include and, most difficult of all, what to leave out. So I offer my apologies now to anyone who feels I should have included more sporting glories, peerless performances or amusing anecdotes, but I could have written five books and still have had enough material for more. Hopefully, this book captures the spirit of LGGS and reveals why it is so important that it shouldn't be forgotten.

The History Lesson

Image 1

Grammar schools were originally established to teach the basics of Latin grammar, essential for anyone wishing to enter government or the church. Although no early records survive, it is thought Leigh Grammar School (LGS) was endowed as an act of charity. There is evidence the school existed in 1592, making it one of the earliest Lancashire grammar schools. Classes were originally held in Leigh Parish Church, but a bequest enabled Headmaster Mr Pilling to build a two-room school in Church Passage in 1719. It was here that some girls became pupils, the tradition being that they were allowed to accompany their brothers to school. They sat on long benches or 'forms', and 'form' became the traditional name for a grammar school class. The Church Passage building fell down in 1919 and a plaque on the church wall now marks its approximate location.

The 1840 Grammar School Act made it lawful for LGS to use the income from its endowment to teach non-classical subjects, but the education it offered was still free. However, when the 1869 Endowed Schools Act allowed it to broaden its curriculum still further, it essentially became a fee-paying academic grammar school. Apart from a few scholarships, it mainly provided a cheaper education and access to university for the sons of middle-class parents who could not afford to send their children to public school.

In 1889 the school purchased a former school building in Railway Road. As the number of scholars continued to increase, Headmaster Mr Leek asked for permission to use the science rooms at the Technical School which had opened in 1894. In 1898 the whole school of forty boys and eighteen girls moved to the Technical School as a temporary measure until more suitable premises could be provided. Mr Leek paid the Technical School seven shillings per student per term for the use of rooms, apparatus, chemicals, cleaning, lighting, heating and attendance. The timetable at the time consisted of: Science (Theoretical Inorganic Chemistry, Practical, Magnetism and Electricity), Geometry, Maths and Arts (Freehand, Model, Light and Shade and Geometrical Drawing).

The 1902 Education Act made county and county borough councils the local education authorities (LEAs) for their areas. They could now subsidise secondary education from the rates, but this created a social divide between the new schools and the endowed grammar schools which received grant-aid from the LEAs. The majority of students at LGS were still fee-paying, but provision was made for a small number of scholarships.

The Technical School now accommodated LGS, the Pupil Teacher Centre and its own classes, so it was hardly surprising that a Board of Education report highlighted the inadequacy of the building. In 1905 Leigh Town Council recommended to the Lancashire Education Committee that the building be expanded to accommodate a grammar school for boys, and that the girls should form a separate school elsewhere. Although the Education Committee agreed the premises could be extended, they rejected the proposal for the girls' school on the grounds that other boroughs would want the same, increasing the cost of secondary education in Lancashire. Instead, the County Architect was instructed to prepare plans for an extension. Leigh Town Council rejected these plans and, as pupil numbers continued to grow, made renewed representations. Finally, the Education Committee reluctantly agreed on the condition that the combined costs of the alterations and a new girls' school did not greatly exceed the estimated cost of the County Architect's plans.

In 1907, the National Board of Education visited the Technical School and concluded it would not be worth spending large sums to extend it to accommodate a mixed school but they would allow it to be used as a temporary base for a secondary school for boys. The County Council refused to accept this report's recommendations but the overcrowding had become so acute that a temporary iron building had to be built on adjoining land. It was agreed that the Board of Education be asked to sanction a separate girls' school on the site.

Meanwhile, the Board of Education was trying to open up grammar schools to children of all social backgrounds on equal terms. The 1907 Education Act required that a proportion of places be offered free on the basis of performance in a competitive scholarship examination;

children whose parents could afford to pay did not need to sit it.

In 1908 Leigh Town Council insisted that building a separate school for girls would be cheaper and stated, 'Public schools for boys and girls of the wealthy classes are not mixed […]. There does not appear to be any reason why the same educational advantages should not be available, so far as is reasonably possible, for Leigh children.' However, they added, 'The curriculum of the girls' school should be widely different from that of the boys''.

The education of girls had been a topic of serious discussion since the 1850s when an increase in the middle classes had led to a greater demand for the education of daughters to make them suitable candidates for marriage. In the Taunton Report of 1868, Miss Davies states, 'The ideal presented to a young girl […] is to be amiable, inoffensive, always ready to give pleasure and to be pleased'. By 1898, there were ninety grammar schools for girls, and teaching was rapidly becoming a popular and respected female profession, particularly after women were allowed to study at a higher level. Owens College, Manchester, part of the federal Victoria University, England's first civic university, allowed women to attend some classes from 1875. But it was not until 1897 that they were finally admitted to most degree examinations (except those in engineering and medicine).

In 1909 LGS was removed from the Board of Education's List of Secondary Schools. A Leigh deputation met with the Board who stressed that the accommodation was only meant to be temporary and unless permanent premises were provided, they were not prepared to renew the grant. The deputation returned to Leigh dejected but quickly arranged a meeting with the school's governors and representatives of the Lancashire Education Committee to discuss their pressing problem. Finally, in 1911, plans were prepared by County Architect Henry Littler II for extensions at the Technical School and a new 'Secondary School for Girls' in Windermere Road. (It wasn't referred to as a grammar school until 1921.) It was to be built in a baroque revivalist style with sash windows, stained glass and classical-style door surrounds. In 1913 D. A. Ablett & Son from Wigan were appointed as builders and, in 1914, a loan was awarded towards the total construction costs of £11,969. The building of the school could finally begin, and this explains the puzzling 1915 date on the ornamental drainpipe casings.

For the next couple of years, the Leigh Education Committee continued to meet to discuss the building works and to authorise the accounts, but the First World War made it increasingly difficult for the contractors to source materials and manpower or to produce an accurate figure for the total costs. So the Committee had to approach the Ministry of Health for permission to borrow more money to meet an estimated excess expenditure.

In December 1920, the Leigh Education Committee adopted the constitution of the Governing Body of the Leigh Girls' Grammar School. It consisted of fifteen persons, later increased to eighteen, at least three of whom had to be women. They were voluntary positions, but each governor had to be nominated and they took their roles very seriously. Their first task was to appoint a headmistress. There were ninety-two applicants, ten of whom were interviewed. The governors selected Miss Nora Caress.

The Headmistresses

Image 2

Miss Nora Caress BSc 1921-27

Born on 13 February 1889 in Winnington, Northwich, Cheshire, Miss Caress was the daughter of a widowed headmaster. After graduating with a degree in Botany from The Victoria University of Manchester, her first position was at Manchester High School (1912-17) where she taught Biology, gained her Teacher's Registration and served in a Red Cross hospital. She then moved to St Paul's Girls' School in London before becoming the first headmistress of

LGGS. She established the Old Girls' Association shortly before she left in 1927 to become headmistress of Wyggeston Grammar School for Girls in Leicester, where she was also one of the founders of the Girls' Training Corps. She retired due to ill health in 1948 and moved to Lyme Regis where she died on 11 July 1961.

Miss Kathleen Elizabeth Perrott MA 1927-42

Born on 27 October 1891 in Watford, Miss Perrott was the daughter of a civil service clerk. A graduate of Newnham College, Cambridge, she gained her Teachers' Registration in 1920. As headmistress of LGGS, she introduced violin classes for Juniors and Seniors, led the Scripture Union and continued Miss Caress' work with the Old Girls' Association. She had been absent for almost two years when she retired due to ill health in 1942. She moved back to Watford, and died on 8 February 1973.

Miss Phyllis Nanney BSc/MSc 1942-47

Born on 26 February 1907 in Wilmslow, Cheshire, Miss Nanney was the daughter of a process- and wood-engraver. She went to Stockport High School for Girls and Manchester High School for Girls then entered Manchester University where she obtained a First Class BSc Honours Chemistry degree in 1928. In 1929 she obtained an MSc degree and, in 1930, took her Diploma of Education at Oxford University. She also gained a certificate in Vocational Guidance Methods from the National Institute of Industrial Psychology. After appointments at Chatham County School, Chislehurst County School and East Sheen County School, she was Chemistry mistress at Clifton High School in Bristol before becoming headmistress at LGGS. She was elected

Founder President of Soroptimist International of Leigh and, together with a small executive team, led the chartering of the club in 1947. She left to become headmistress of Leyton County High School for Girls and died in Hereford in 1999.

Miss Muriel Isabella Shanks BA 1948-54

Born on 3 April 1910 in Newcastle, Miss Shanks was the daughter of an insurance clerk. She was brought up in Carlisle where she was Head Girl at Carlisle County High School for Girls and went on to study Classics at Manchester University. She taught in Middleton and was Senior Classics Mistress at Kings Norton Grammar School for Girls in Birmingham before becoming headmistress at LGGS. The LGGS magazine reveals, 'A Northerner by birth and education, she understood the difficulties and the potentialities of the area and the people […]. She combined her own extremely exacting academic standards of a radical mind with a great understanding and sensitivity plus a real sense of humour. The girls at school were always her first concern. Her intellectual ability and dignity earned her great respect because she appreciated and encouraged individual values and talents in others.' She was an accomplished hockey player and Lady Captain at Leigh Tennis Club. She introduced the annual Carol Service, encouraged the founding of the Film Society and stimulated an interest in current affairs with morning talks. She left to become headmistress of The Park School, Preston, and later became Principal of the Sixth Form College, Preston. She was actively involved in public life, particularly with Age Concern, and, when she retired, planned to travel. Sadly, she died aged seventy as a result of head injuries in a car accident in Scotland on 13 September 1980.

Miss Marjorie Hulme BA 1954-61

Born on 30 November 1922 in Hulme, Miss Hulme was the daughter of a widowed elementary school headmaster. She attended Bury Grammar School where she was Head Girl in 1940. From 1941 to 1944 she attended Girton College, Cambridge, where she studied Mathematics and gained a 'blue' for rowing. She taught at Collegiate School, Blackpool and at Wade Deacon Grammar School in Widnes before becoming headmistress of LGGS. She managed to secure many improvements to the building, including a new Physics laboratory and a new set of classrooms, and came up with other inventive ways to accommodate the growing number of girls. She left in 1961 to become headmistress at Withington Girls' School and, on her retirement in 1985, became the Chairman of the Greater Manchester Educational Trust.

Miss Muriel Swindells BSc/DipEd 1961-74

Born on 2 November 1914 in Rochdale, Miss Swindells attended Oldham High School, a mixed grammar school. She was one of only four girls studying Chemistry in her year at Manchester University in 1934. The male students offered to pay the girls to prepare their chemicals but she refused. She was in the Choral Society and played the violin and, having been a Girl Guide herself, became lieutenant of a company. She taught at St Albans Grammar School for Girls and The Grammar School for Girls in Bridgwater, Somerset, but found travelling very difficult under blackout conditions so looked for a position nearer to her home town, Oldham. She joined LGGS as Science mistress in 1946, becoming the first permanent Deputy Head in 1958, and the first member of staff promoted to Headmistress in 1961. She became a member of the Panel of Science Teachers in South East Lancashire, and gave lectures and led discussions on science teaching at meetings of the Association of Women Science Teachers, North West Branch. She organised many walking holidays and ran the school Guide company with Dorothy Bannister. She was Captain, District Commissioner and Division Commissioner for Leigh and District Girl Guides as well as County Adviser for 'Handicapped' Guides and a County Vice-President. She was also a member of Soroptimist International of Leigh and did excellent work as President during her year in office. When she retired in 1973, she continued to be involved in education as a governor of Leigh Church of England Infants and Junior Schools and enjoyed cycling and walking with her best friend, Dorothy Bannister. When her health started to fail she moved in with Dorothy and died unexpectedly in October 1993 in Hope Hospital aged 78.

Miss Beryl Smart BSc 1974-76

Born on 8 March 1933 in Widnes, the daughter of a leather tanner, Miss Smart graduated in 1955 with a joint degree in Botany and Zoology from Sheffield University, and was appointed as an assistant teacher of Biology at LGGS. Initially, she continued to live with her parents and sister in Widnes, travelling to and from Leigh in her blue Austin A30, but she moved to Culcheth in 1968. She played for the Chester Ladies Hockey Club but suffered a back injury which caused her trouble in later life. Despite this, she was an energetic and enthusiastic teacher in and out of the classroom and was known for her patience, poise and sense of humour. She organised regular Biology fieldwork excursions and became involved in many of the school societies. She revived the Film Society, organised the

Scientific and Naturalist Societies, was involved in the Debating Society, and accompanied several school trips abroad. For many years she organised the Charity Committee, and once travelled with Oxfam to see some of their projects in operation. She took part in the school's stage shows as a producer, lighting expert and actress, and encouraged regular musical and dramatic productions in school and local drama and arts festivals. Beside her work at LGGS, she gave service to the Schools Council and one of the major teachers' unions. She was appointed Deputy Head in 1961 and when Miss Swindells retired everyone was delighted she was chosen as the seventh Headmistress. Under her leadership the school's curriculum and outlook broadened and she helped staff, pupils and their parents, to feel part of the local community. She became Vice President, then President, of the National Association of Assistant Headmistresses and a Fellow of the British Institute of Management. When LGGS closed she became Vice Principal of Leigh College for twelve months before becoming the first female head teacher of Canon Slade School, Bolton. When she retired she first became a churchwarden and lay preacher then was ordained as a deacon and a priest. She died on 26 August 2013 aged 80.

Miss CARESS
1921–1927.

Image 3

Miss PERROTT
1928–1942

Image 4

25

Image 5

Image 6

Image 7

Image 8

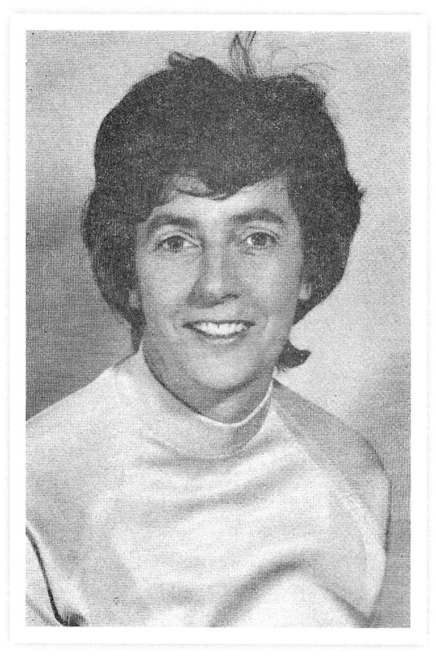

Image 9

The Head Girls

Image 10

1923-25	Alice Baron
1925-26	Mildred Cullen
1926-27	Mildred Cullen
1927-28	Edith Caldwell
1928-29	Constance Groves
1929-30	Margaret Beirne
1930-31	Helen Ward
1931-32	Elizabeth Stott
1932-33	Bessie Howarth
1933-34	May Jolley
1934-35	Alice Blundell
1935-36	Dorothy Bannister
1936-37	Bessie Tyldesley
1936-37	Kitty Haworth
1937-38	Bessie Povah
1938-39	Margaret Owen
1939-40	Mary Osselton
1939-40	Joan Bullough
1939-40	Helen Clegg
1940-41	Vera Darwell
1941-42	Kathleen Yates
1942-43	Irene Massey
1943-44	Doreen Richards
1944-45	Joan Barnes
1945-46	Eleanor Pharaoh
1946-47	Ethel Smith
1947-48	Ursula Lee
1948-49	Doris Johnson
1949-50	Nancy Baxter
1950-51	Dorothy Leather
1951-52	Dorothy Hope
1952-53	Shirley Mills
1953-54	Barbara Mercer

1954-55	Brenda M. Booth
1955-56	Dorothy Chadwick
1956-57	Marian Seddon
1957-58	Audrey Seddon
1958-59	Jean Mort
1959-60	Marie Porter
1960-61	Barbara Webster
1961-62	Barbara Lee
1962-63	Gloria Broom
1963-64	Margaret Bond
1964-65	Kathryn Sarginson
1965-66	Sheila Hazlitt
1966-67	Susan Shawcross
1967-68	Ann Matthias
1968-69	Anne Sizer
1969-70	Susan Dornan
1970-71	Gillian Pritchard
1971-72	Judith Page
1972-73	Carolyn Woodburn
1973-74	Anita Brierley
1974-75	Ann Eccleshare
1975-76	Pauline Dobbs

The 1920s

Image 11

Headmistresses: *Miss Caress 1921-27 / Miss Perrott 1927-42*

Contributors to this chapter: *Vera Chapman (née Leigh, 1921-27), Ethel Timperley (née Grundy, 1920s), Dorothy Ratcliffe (née Horrocks, 1925-26), E. Wharton (née Lathwaite, 1929-34), Helen Ward (Head Girl 1930-31), Marian Matthews (née Bingham), Lena Tickle (née Parry,*

1926-33), Gladys May Thomson (1919-21), Alice Baron (1921-25. First Head Girl, 1923-5).

*

At the Governors' Meeting in June 1921, it was estimated the school would consist of 240 to 250 girls divided into eight forms: 'The minimum staff [...] would be ten assistant mistresses with probably some part-time assistance for domestic and physical training. It is clear that a considerable number of the present staff [*at LGS*] will expect to be transferred to the new school and it is suggested that the following mistresses should be so transferred if they themselves are willing: Mrs Williams, Miss Fullerton, Miss Rodgers, Miss Crowcroft, Miss Clough, Miss Carr, Miss Calderbank, Miss Woolstenholme.' Miss Woolstenholme turned down the offer so it was decided that a further three appointments would be needed and Miss Caress was asked to help draw up advertisements for them. These would include a full-time instructress in Physical Training and an Art teacher. Mr E. France was also appointed as Music teacher, and an advertisement was drawn up for a man and his wife to be caretakers for £5 per week. Six couples were subsequently interviewed and Mr Albert Ward and Mrs A Ward appointed. Their duties would include 'cleaning the inside of all windows not less than six times a year and washing all their own dusters', but Mr Ward clearly didn't find this too onerous as he stayed at LGGS until 1939. His assistant caretaker, Mrs Harrison, was to stay even longer until 1953.

Miss Caress recommended Miss Huish for Science, Miss Chandler for Classics, Miss Wareing for Maths and Miss McNaughton for PT. Miss Ashcroft was also appointed for Needlework, temporarily for one year. Most of the teachers were either already teaching at LGS or recommended by Miss Caress, so she would have had confidence in their abilities and experience. They were all appointed under the Burnham Scale, the first step towards standardisation of teachers' salaries. With the exception of Mrs Williams, all the staff members were spinsters as they were expected to give up work if they got married. It wasn't until 1940 that Miss Currie was allowed to keep her job after she became Mrs Griffin, and that was only because there was a war on.

Despite the many years of construction, there was a lot of last-minute work to prepare the school. But according to the school's minute book the newly appointed staff, 'from September 14th to the opening day worked unfailing and with the most complete good humour at such heavy and dirty jobs as unpacking crates of apparatus and materials, unpacking and carrying furniture, etc'. Sadly this didn't include the Staffroom chairs or couches which only arrived in July 1922. One of these original Staffrooms was located in what was to later to become the Headmistress' Study, whilst the headmistress resided next to the front door in what was later to become the Office, with the School Secretary in the tiny adjoining room. The main entrance to the school was, at that time, via double gates opening onto Honiston Street which ran parallel to what was then the Hall, later the Gym.

Even before the school opened, the governors recorded 'that the county be asked to make early arrangements for the provision of additional accommodation to provide for the increase in number which will take place in September of next year'. The Leigh Town Council Clerk met with the Borough Surveyor with a view to obtaining a field suitable for sports, the nearest being in Pennington. 'Blackfields', between Grange Street and the railway embankment off St Helens Road, was finally purchased in 1925. In the meantime, games were held at the Parish Church Field off Platt Fold Road. There were no changing facilities so the girls had to leave their belongings on the grass.

The school was officially opened on 11 November by the Rt. Hon. H. E. Lewis MP. On her retirement in 1950, Miss Wareing recalled the opening ceremony, 'Ward and I held a cord across the bottom corridor so that everyone had to go clockwise round to the Hall, now the Gymnasium. And how dirty we were, Leigh dust falling heavily on all our clothes as we unpacked books, etc and workmen still busy! But what wonderful caretakers we had.' Vera remembers presenting a bouquet to Miss Caress at the opening ceremony.

LGGS finally opened on 22 September 1921 with 252 pupils, 153 of which transferred from LGS. 114 of the girls came from Leigh with the rest from Earlestown, Atherton, Tyldesley, Lowton, Astley, Kenyon, Newton, Culcheth, Burtonwood, Westhoughton, Croft, Winwick, Chequerbent and even Barton Moss. The new school attracted pupils from a wide catchment area because it was single sex, and in a town that, at the time, had excellent transport links with a tram system and two train stations. But, even on public transport, the girls were expected to conform to school rules, as Vera recalls, 'Train girls hadn't to dominate conversation on the train nor had tram girls.'

Ninety-seven of the girls were fee-paying which meant they didn't have to sit an entrance exam. Vera again, 'The fees were two pounds and two shillings until 1923 when they went up, but they were still under three pounds when my sister joined the school.' The rest of the girls attended via free places (County Bursaries, County Junior Exhibition, France's Scholarships) or as 'others'. Girls were expected to commit to their studies and could be asked to pay a penalty fee if they broke their School Agreement. If they wanted to be released from the Agreement early, e.g. to start work, their parents had to write a letter to the school's governors for permission, which was granted only in exceptional circumstances.

Ethel remembers, 'When I was twelve, Lancashire County Council offered a few five-year bursaries to selected pupils and the headmaster put my name forward to take the exam. Mr Parkinson came to see my parents for their consent. My father, being at home from work, agreed against my mother's wishes. I sat the exam along with another girl and I passed and was offered a place.' Her mother, like a lot of parents at that time, may have wondered what the point was of educating her daughter when her main aim would be to marry and have children. However, there would also have been financial concerns as Ethel recalls, 'My days at the school were very happy, apart from the shortage of cash to buy all my textbooks. There were many tears shed when I asked for money and it was refused, and I had to make excuses to the teachers until I could eventually get the cash.' All girls had to buy their own books which were sold, under direction of the headmistress, at cost price.

Another major expense was the uniform which, at that time, was a continuation of what the girls had worn at LGS. In winter, this consisted of a navy serge gym slip with four box pleats front and back and three buttons on each shoulder. It had to measure three or four inches off the ground when kneeling down. This was worn with a square-necklined white shirt, an optional striped silk tie of navy and red, and a navy woven braid girdle or sash, the knot of which had to be tied a particular way. There was also a navy V-neck pullover with a band of red around the bottom and the cuffs. Long black woollen stockings were worn in winter, held up by suspenders, usually sewn onto a liberty bodice. White socks with black shoes were stipulated in summer. Outdoor shoes had to be removed on arrival and deposited in shoe bags on pegs in the Cloakroom. They were replaced with rubber-heeled 'house shoes' to be worn around the building until girls went on trips, to games or back home. When outside, the girls had to wear navy blue straw hats with a large brim which used to wilt. Dorothy remembers, 'When this got rained on the crown rose to a point and we were called the "Sally Army".' In summer the hat was replaced by a panama worn with a blue check dress, navy blazer and gloves. E. Wharton recalls, 'Gloves had to be worn in the street. No eating sweets in the street either. We were not allowed to wear clips in our hair, a slide or a hair band had to be worn.' There was no gym kit. Instead, girls wore their blouses tucked into the obligatory black knickers.

After a couple of years in charge, Miss Perrott made some changes to the uniform. The white shirt was replaced with a cream round-collared blouse worn without a tie and, in summer 1924, the panama hat gave way to a navy serge cap. This had fabric gathered into a cuff at the back and sides like the Women's Land Army cap. The navy blue straw hat of winter was later replaced by a navy blue velour hat.

According to Helen, 'The school crest of the red stag and the *Swift and Sure* motto was chosen by Miss Caress from a series of drawings made by my uncle, Tom Yates, the architect.' Miss Caress herself stated, 'As the school was to be a new one, with no past traditions, and was, moreover, to serve a wider area than the town of Leigh, it seemed undesirable to use local history to provide us with a pseudo-heraldic crest. A more attractive badge would be one that expressed the vigorous LIFE, which we hoped would be, from the first, characteristic of the young School. A trotting stag seemed to be the embodiment of vitality, of courage, strength and grace. The coat-of-arms of the borough of

Leigh has at its foot the inscription *Aequo pede propera* – a literal translation of which would be rendered *Hasten with equal foot*; this rendering we paraphrased as *Swift and Sure* and so obtained the motto which we use at the foot of our badge, and for which the trotting stag is again a pictorial representation.'

E. Wharton remembers the school cap had 'a metal badge on the front in blue enamel with a red deer on it.' Most of the school uniform could be purchased from *Danby's* in Market Street but a firm from Manchester came to the school every year to measure girls up for blazers and hats. Miss Wareing used to deal with all the orders and payments and kept meticulous records. Each item had to have a *Cash's* name tape sewn neatly inside it, and there were sporadic inspections to make sure each girl had complied.

Another cost was school dinners, originally eaten at tables in the 'Dining Room' of Rooms 11 and 12. In 1921 the charge was 9d a head so some girls went home for lunch or brought their own. Marian remembers, 'In a little pantry off the Kitchen two girls were delegated each term to make hot Bovril or cocoa or hot milk to augment the sandwiches. Dinner girls had washing-up duty.' Initially, the dinners were supplied by the National Kitchens, a state-backed local business created to alleviate food poverty, but the school had to request the installation of a hot oven to keep them warm.

The school followed the Public School system in that there was no First form. Instead the forms were Second, Third, Fourth, Upper Fourth, Fifth, Sixth and Upper Sixth. However, there was no Sixth Form when LGGS first opened as the Fifths had stayed on at LGS. The year groups were divided into *Alpha* or *Arts and Science*, depending on the girls' choices of subjects and their grades. Within their forms, girls were encouraged to arrange their own activities including picnics and fundraising. There was an early campaign to provide a fiction section for the school Library, which resulted in lots of diminutive saleswomen selling their wares to raise the necessary funds. These included photos, painted glassware and even tickets to parties and a performance by a jazz band. Incredibly, the school did not have a library until 1929 when Room 9 (upstairs next to the east staircase) was made into a makeshift one. The Library had large windows with a view blocked by the Staffroom, Tax Office, parish church and houses. According to the school magazine, 'Shields and cups were kept in there but were not well polished. It was the general bureau and enquiry office of the school and also used as a form room.' The upper school forms helped to catalogue the new Library with no shortage of volunteers.

There were approximately thirty girls in each form and most lessons lasted around forty minutes. Lena particularly enjoyed acting short plays in English and doing dissection in Biology, but not her three lots of subject homework every school night. Assembly was held in the Gym (which was originally the Hall) every morning before lessons began. It lasted around thirty minutes and the girls marched in to music played by Miss Pilling on the piano. Seconds sat at the front, then in order of year group up to the Sixth Form at the back. The girls sat cross-legged on the parquet floor with staff seated on chairs down one side. Sixth-Formers had a rota to read the lesson at the lectern on the platform and if a girl could play the piano reasonably well she was put on a rota to play the hymn and the closing march back to lessons. One girl was elected to take the Headmistress' hymn book to the table on the small platform and this would herald her entry into the assembly, at which the whole school stood up. There was a hymn, a prayer, a reading and then any notices. In later years, a slot was introduced during which Sixth-Formers had to prepare and deliver a short talk on current affairs. The few Roman Catholic girls who attended the school were excused from assembly and supervised by prefects.

After assembly, the Gym was used for PE, while netball, tennis and hockey took place in the playground or at the Parish Church Field until the new sports field was finally ready around 1928. Amongst the traditional sports, the annual Sports Day also included the more unusual Overhead Bean Bag Race, Three-Legged Egg and Spoon Race, Horse and Driver Race, Slow Cycle Race, Potato Race and Guides' Tent Pitching Competition. All followed by lemonade and biscuits. The girls also went swimming at Leigh Public Baths in Silk Street.

E. Wharton remembers the girls had to walk in 'crocodiles' outside school, while inside, 'There were strict rules about moving from one classroom to another, single file along the corridors and stairs and no talking. Woe betide anyone caught running. A prefect was stationed at the top of the stairs to see everyone behaved.' The behaviour of the girls was also closely monitored in the playground as Vera vividly recalls, 'When I was in Form IIa, a few girls were talking to some LGS boys through the school railings in the dinner hour. When they came in class afterwards all went quiet as we looked at Miss Clough's face. Our form motto was *Loyalty* and there was a deathly silence as she tore it up. It was a long time before any of us smiled again.'

The school's inadequate size was apparent, and building began again almost immediately. A letter was written by the governors in 1923 to the Director of Education for the County regarding an extension and, soon after, a single storey wood and brick 'New Wing' was added at the rear of the building. This provided a proper Dining Hall, a new entrance for the girls, an additional laboratory and a bigger Staffroom. In the meantime, some classes were held in the

Primitive Methodist School on Windermere Road. The new extension was celebrated in March 1924 with an Open Day including an exhibition of work and singing and dancing entertainment by the girls for their parents.

At that time, the school curriculum included Scripture, English, Maths, History, German, French, Classics, Science, Chemistry, Biology, Physics, Botany, Cookery, Needlework, Music and PE. As stated in the 1928 summer issue of the school magazine, 'In these days of female emancipation it is true that we are rather prone to neglect the domestic arts.' Ethel remembers how competitive girls could be in classes, 'A girl called Edith also passed the bursary exam from the C of E School. We were friendly rivals because she, like me, was rather clever and she used to gloat if she did better than me. When we entered our fourth year, Edith and I both chose Science. We both did Chemistry but whilst Edith did Biology, I did Physics, a subject that I liked but found very hard to understand. I had a schoolgirl crush on Miss Harker, the Science teacher, and so, of course, worked much harder for her. She also taught Physics and as there were only six of us in the class, you would've thought that we would all do very well. But, when it came to the School Certificate exam, I only got a pass. We all took six subjects to matriculate and I had Credits in Maths, History and Chemistry but only Passes in Physics, French and English. This was not good enough to get me to college, but Edith got six credits, so you can imagine how she crowed. My results were a great shock to me. I walked out of the school absolutely devastated and never went back. I missed the school Prize Giving as I was ill in bed with a bad dose of flu, so I didn't even get to go up on the platform to receive my School Certificate and my School Prize for Chemistry.'

The UK School Certificate was introduced as a standard educational qualification in 1918 and was usually taken at the age of sixteen. Each subject was graded as Fail, Pass, Credit or Distinction and six passes, including English and Maths were needed to matriculate. Those who failed could retake the exam, and those who passed could stay on at school to take the Higher School Certificate at eighteen.

Another girl who didn't collect her School Certificate was Gladys, 'Along with the other girls who had had two years of LGS, I should have sat for a matriculation exam in July 1922 but Miss Caress decided to postpone it for twelve months, believing that more girls would pass. So some girls left after four years without an exam. I stayed on but the only time I ever went back after leaving the school was to receive my matrix certificate.'

Alice had a more positive experience, 'I am very grateful for the early training I received at LGGS. It was there that I learned the necessity for hard work and the satisfaction to be derived from serving the community. Also, during my schooldays, many interests were established which have enriched my life.'

There were certainly lots of opportunities to develop new interests outside the curriculum. There were two Girl Guides troops (3rd A Leigh and 5th Leigh) based at the school and led by the staff. They took the Guides camping at Worsley New Hall and to a rally at Belle Vue in 1929, which was also attended by Princess Mary. The Captain of the 3rd Leigh Guides was the aptly name Art teacher Miss Drew who also led the Literary Society. Members put on dramatic productions and the Debating Section discussed in 1929 whether or not 'Capital Punishment should be abolished'. There were many other groups and societies including The Philanthropical Society, later The School Guild, which held an annual party for the children of Leigh Union Workhouse. There was a school branch of the League of Nations, a Scientific Society, and a school orchestra which arranged a

Musical and Dramatic Evening in 1928 with the LGS Orchestra to raise funds for the school Library. The Scripture Union started in 1928 with 200 members. They read a short passage of the Bible every day and sent gifts to a school in Kenya. Even the School Secretary, Mrs Holden, led a small weekly gathering of pupils in her office for religious discussion assisted, when possible, by Miss Perrott. After-school lectures were regularly arranged including 'Bubbles and their Uses' which was also attended by the Upper School of LGS. The school magazine first went to press in spring 1926, edited by Miss Hyatt for many years. There were even activities during the summer holidays including University Women's Camps for Schoolgirls which several pupils attended and reported having had a thoroughly jolly time.

In May 1927 Miss Caress, after establishing a lot of the school's traditions, offered her resignation. The following month, the governors noted in their minutes that they had each received a letter signed by eight members of staff with reference to the appointment of the next headmistress. The contents of the letter are not revealed, and the staff are not named, but they were ordered to withdraw the letter and apologise which they duly did. Eight candidates were then interviewed for the post, including at least one member of staff, Miss Wareing, but a Miss Mary Louise Holloway was appointed. However, she offered her resignation in July and the post was offered to another of the candidates, Miss Ethel Strachan Henny. She must have turned the offer down as Miss B. A. Kennett, a retired headmistress from Perse Girls' School, Cambridge, was appointed as temporary Headmistress for one term until Miss Perrott finally arrived in spring 1928.

*

Most Talked-About Staff:

Miss Marion Wareing BSc, Head of Maths & Higher Maths, 1921-50

Although she was considered a patient teacher who always gave lots of praise, she also expected the best and would not tolerate apathy or laziness. She was Chairman of the Scientific Society, and the official recorder on Sports Days. A familiar sight on her bicycle, she once had a cycling accident on holiday in Norway and was off school for a term. She was interviewed for the position of headmistress when Miss Caress left, but was unsuccessful. She maintained a keen interest in Old Girls, welcoming them back warmly, and was a keen member of the Old Girls' Association (OGA). She was also a National Union of Teachers (NUT) representative and attended meetings. When she retired she donated a magazine shelf for the Library and gave a Christmas tree to the school every year.

Miss L. M. Clough, Scripture & English, 1921-43

As form mistress, she encouraged her form to polish the tops of their desks. According to the school magazine, 'Miss Clough likes us to be as bright as possible.' Her cupboard was full of relics and treasures including 'a fine horse-hair brush with which she whisked countless bits of grit from Second Form eyes – and other eyes as well.' She had a good sense of humour and used to impersonate the Lancashire accents of her pupils. A keen Methodist, she led the school Scripture Union. Described as a friend to the girls, she was much missed when she retired.

Miss Jane Fullerton, Maths & RE, 1921-35

Nicknamed 'Fuzzy', she gave a lot of time and energy to the 'Book Room' or stationery cupboard. The school magazine states, 'Her sympathy and practical help were always at the disposal of both girls and staff, and although delinquents had good reason to see her sharp eyes and telling comments, they were ever the first to own that she had their welfare very much at heart. The energy with which she applied herself to anything she undertook was an inspiration to all and put many a younger, fainter heart to shame [...]. She has always been a woman of her word – even when keeping her promise meant standing on her head before a triumphant class. Who but she, with her ready wit, would have thought of the expedient of writing the words *my head* on paper and suddenly standing on that?' On her retirement, she donated books, rock and mineral specimens, and fossils to the Library, awarded a Progress Prize in her name and became a keen member of the OGA.

Notable Events

In 1922 the school's Health Record stated there were only fourteen cases of infectious illness, including measles, scarlet fever and influenza. However, Dorothy remembers, 'There was a smallpox scare and the whole school was lined up with their sleeves rolled back to be vaccinated.' In a time of poor living conditions, it was noted that the physical condition of many of the girls had been improved through gym exercises, sports and school dinners.

In 1927 Mildred Cullen was first on the External Examination Successes Honours Board with a Lancashire County Council Major Scholarship.

In 1929, at the November 11th Founder's Day Service, Alderman Ashworth, who was resigning as Chairman of the

Governors, asked for the girls to be given a day's holiday in celebration of the school's birthday.

The Old Girls' Association

The inaugural meeting was held on 20 July 1927, in the School Hall, with Miss Caress in the chair. She wanted to see an Association established before she left the school. Its aims were:
- to aid the growth and influence of the school in all lawful ways
- to bind together the past and the present
- to give help to any former members of the school who may be in danger, necessity or tribulation.
  Miss Caress was made the first Honorary Vice-President. There was a committee of twelve, made up of eight girls (including the Head Girl) and four staff, and included a Secretary and a Treasurer. There were two general meetings a year at Christmas and Midsummer. Subscription was four shillings, which included two annual school magazines and supper at the general meetings, plus a one shilling entrance fee. A cheaper rate was charged for 'country' members who couldn't attend the meetings. Life membership was two and a half guineas which were invested in government stock. Girls had to have attended the school for three years to be full members. If they had attended for less time, they could be an associate but they couldn't vote until they had been a member for three years. To encourage more girls to join, members of the committee were asked to act as 'whippers-in' for their district, and congratulations were sent when any old girls got married. By the third meeting, there were 148 members and there was talk of a membership badge even though the actual name of the Association hadn't yet been decided on. In 1929 they voted on a name from a choice of:

The Old Girls' Guild, Leigh Old Girls, The Second Leighians (LGS Old Boys were The Leighians), Leigh Old Grammarians or The Old Girls' Association. The latter name was adopted. Thomas Fattorini Ltd, designers and makers of emblematic jewellery, were asked to create a badge design which was discussed but soon abandoned. As the school and its Old Girls were relatively young at this time, and many were still living locally, the Association decided to hold monthly meetings. There were also regular tennis matches held at the school field, and netball games on the school courts, though they had to get changed in the bike shed. A tennis tournament was arranged between old and current girls with Eau de Cologne as prizes. At the general meetings, the Gym was used for dancing and the Dining Room for supper, and they closed by singing the school song.

Notable Alumni

Margaret Beirne (Head Girl LGGS 1929-30), Lady Barker of St Helens. Her husband was diplomat Sir William Barker KCMG OBE.

Image 12

Image 13

Image 14

Image 15

The 1930s

Image 16

Headmistress: *Miss Perrott 1927-42*

Contributors to this chapter: *Joyce Lyon (née Rhoden, 1930s), Muriel Hayes (née Mason, 1926-31), Kathleen Langhorne (née Vaudrey, 1930-37), Mary 'Evelyn' Dickinson (née Shaw, 1938-43), G. Marsden (1939-44), Nora Parker (née Worsley, 1937-44), Doris Sexton (née Parry, 1932-38), Sadie Lee (1937-41), Constance M. Taylor (née France, 1932-34).*

*

W.H. Leek had introduced a house system at LGS, but it doesn't appear to have been implemented at LGGS until the 1930s. The 1935 school magazine explains, 'it is fitting that the Houses should be named after people of the North, famous in industry, science and literature.' The House names and colours were Arkwright (the inventor), red, whose captain was Dorothy Bannister, Bronte (the novelist), blue, Cavendish (the scientist), yellow, and Mackenzie (the cardiologist), green.

Joyce remembers, 'Each House had a House Captain and a Deputy. There was also a House Representative from each form. We all wore a flash on the left-hand side of our gym slip to denote our House. No other badges were allowed except the Scripture Union lamp. There were House hockey and netball teams and inter-House matches umpired by prefects especially on Sports Day. Form period was once a week in the Junior forms, for name inspections, desk tidying and voting of officers such as Form Captain, House and society representatives. We also stuck stars and blobs on House charts. A silver star was for good work, a brown blob was a disorder mark given, for example, for losing property. A black blob was a misconduct mark which was very bad.'

Muriel remembers getting a dreaded misconduct mark when raising money for charity, 'I think it must've been for Miss Perrott's sister who was a missionary. I seem to remember her visiting the school and telling us about her work. I was given pencils to sell which were the colour of the Houses with the name of the House on. Off I went selling them but I let most of the pencils go before collecting the money. What a worrying time this was for me, no way could I get all the money in. I couldn't sleep I was so worried. In the end the mistress had to be told. I think I'd cleared the price of the pencils but with little profit and for all my worrying I was given a misconduct mark. It broke my heart and it taught me a lesson. I think if this happened today the child would tell their parents and they would put everything right, but it wasn't easy to do that in the thirties.'

Joyce continues, 'Each mistress had a tear off paper 'chitty' block on which good and bad marks were written, dated and signed. The Form Mistress gave out stars and demerits on production of the chitty. They were stuck opposite your name on the House list on the Form Room wall and also entered at the bottom of your report.' At the end of the year, the point score for each House was arrived at by collating the number of silver stars throughout the school and subtracting the disorder and misconduct marks. The Harker House Trophy was a statuette of a schoolgirl holding onto her hat in the wind.'

Special girdles of House colours were awarded, after one year in the school. According to the school magazine, these were given to 'certain girls who, besides being especially good at Gymnastics and at Games, also show all-round merit both in work and personal character. The girdle is only retained so long as is that record is maintained. The narrow girdle of the Junior School is replaced by a broad one when the owner reaches Form V if she still has the right to wear it.'

The much prized self-coloured girdle was tied on by the headmistress during the final assembly of the year. Meanwhile, the general navy girdle was now produced with a zigzag in the House colour but was worn over the same style of gym slip. However, at some point, the round-collared cream blouse had been replaced with a cream Tobralco blouse which had a collar with pointed ends, between which the navy and red striped tie, if worn, had to fit neatly. The sleeves had double cuffs but cufflinks weren't allowed. Instead, girls had to fasten them with two buttons on elastic. If hair was shoulder length it had to be worn with an Alice band, and if it was long, it had to be plaited or fastened back with a slide.

Shoes still had to be black, preferably lace-ups. 'House shoes', low-heeled black slippers with a bar and button fastening, still had to be changed into on arrival at school, and girls had to make their own shoe bag in brown Crashor Holland linen and embroider it with their name in their House colour. The bag was hung on a coat peg and the outdoor shoes put into a wire locker beneath. School books were to be carried in a satchel. Girls still had to wear white socks in summer and long black stockings in winter. Kathleen recalls the problems they caused, 'How I hated swimming lessons. Trying to follow the instructions shouted from the side by the Games mistress. Then, after about fifteen minutes, came the scramble to get dressed, and here entered the real villain of the piece – black woollen stockings. Just try pulling those horrible things over half-dry legs and contorting yourself in the space of a sentry box to fasten suspenders. Afterwards, back at school, lessons were spent most uncomfortably with itchy legs and wet locks.'

Girls played games such as hockey in their heavy serge tunics which they then had to wear for the rest of the day, without access to a shower, until these were finally provided towards the end of the decade. For PE they wore their blouse tucked into their regulation black school knickers which had elastic in the leg hems and were worn over an additional pair of white knickers. As Evelyn says, 'We never knew why but they did check.' Slip-on gym shoes had leather uppers, crepe soles and elastic at the instep, and cost four shillings and sixpence per pair. The navy blue blazer with *Swift and Sure* on the breast pocket was originally worn under a navy blue gabardine mac, but after the war started girls were allowed to wear any dark coat. In winter, girls wore a navy blue felt or velour 'bucket' hat with a navy and red striped hatband bearing the *Swift and Sure* emblem, and gloves. As Muriel remembers, 'We always had to wear our gloves and hat. I think the wearing of gloves stayed with me all through my life and most probably did with most of the other girls. I don't feel dressed to this day without them.' G. Marsden remembers, 'I once got a disorder mark for being seen carrying my gloves instead of wearing them.'

In summer, the blazer was worn over a blue and white small-check dress, and accompanied by white ankle socks, black shoes and a panama hat with the LGGS hatband. Nora remembers, 'Even on the warmest days you were not allowed to eat ice cream on the streets if you were wearing school uniform.' But Muriel and her friends, like many girls after her, were prepared to take a risk, 'We weren't allowed to eat while wearing our school uniform but a cheap sweet shop opened at the bus stop near the Town Hall. One girl used to keep watch whilst we went indoors. It was woe betide anyone who was caught eating sweets by a prefect or member of staff.' A misconduct mark, perhaps?

Once girls reached the Sixth Form they were allowed to wear a pure shantung silk blouse with the school tie and a plain navy skirt instead of the hated tunic or gym slip. As the school had been operational for a number of years by then, girls could buy some secondhand articles of uniform and books which helped to keep costs down. Evelyn remembers, 'We were canny. We would find a girl who had looked after her books and ask her to sell them to us.' Girls were able to make one uniform item, their Magyar-style cookery apron, in their Needlework class. Doris recalls they were also 'taught to darn socks and do smocking, and we made underskirts, the top joined to the bottom using fagoting.' Evelyn made a pair of pyjamas, 'You had to draft the pattern and sew it.'

Muriel tells of when every girl in the school took part in a sewing project, 'We helped to sew and embroider a large mural which was framed and hung up behind the staff table. I seem to remember it was a Spring scene with lambs on it.' The embroidered panel was designed by Miss Drew and another Art teacher Miss Tuson, and the Domestic Science staff helped to supervise the stitching.

The Dining Room was to become a place of many rituals and traditions. Small individual bottles of milk were collected from here during the morning break. Dinner tickets, 10d each in books of five, were purchased from the School Office at a certain time each week. The girl's name had to be written on each ticket which she then posted in a box on the ground floor corridor each morning before lessons began. Lunch was served from 12 till 1.15pm in the Hall which temporarily became the Dining Room. The girls sat in groups of eight at trestle tables covered with white cloths. Those who brought their own sandwiches sat at tables specially reserved for them. Evelyn recalls, 'Sandwiches had to be in a white bag with a name tape and you had to put it on the table ready in the morning. Once, my mum had forgotten to wash it and I had to go and see Miss Perrott who told me it wasn't hygienic and not to do it again.' Nora says, 'The staff dined on a platform at one end of the Hall. Either the Headmistress or one appointed mistress was in charge. When the staff arrived, the whole Hall was silent and Grace was said before we resumed our seats and appointed servers from each table who went to the Kitchen hatches to bring the food. It was a special privilege to be chosen to serve the staff. I think it was the Fifth-Formers who would be selected for the honour of collecting a huge trolley from the Kitchen laden with tureens, gravy boats, plates, etc. One had to mount the steps to the platform with great care and then service the staff in a certain order and, of course, from a certain side. The pupils were allowed to talk quietly but, if noise levels rose, the authoritarian tinkle of a fork on a glass stopped everything. Sometimes the rest of the meal was eaten in silence.' Girls were not allowed to leave the school at dinnertime unless it was to go home to eat.

In 1937, Miss Perrott asked for a leave of absence for the summer term to go to India. In her absence, Miss Marlow was appointed Acting Headmistress and Miss Steele became Second Mistress.

In 1938 a new wireless set, a radiogram, was installed in the Dining Room. At the same time, a further two-storey brick-built flat-roofed extension was added at the Leigh Fire Station end of the building, providing extra classrooms. Unfortunately, it also spoiled the external symmetry of the exterior, and the different floor levels inside meant the new rooms had to be accessed by steps. In September Miss Perrott took possession of her new room on the south side of the building, and the staff moved out to the 'New Wing' or 'Annexe' which now had showers and, according to the school magazine, 'a complete set of new curtains made for the school stage, comprising a buff backcloth, buff "legs", and a light blue Traverse curtain. The position of the latter now provides us with an "apron stage", which will be very useful in Shakespearean productions'. The back wall of the Library was fitted out with shelves to accommodate a loan of one hundred books from the County Library, and the Geography Room received green and black curtains and a screen so that lantern lectures could be held there.

Nora vividly remembers that, around this time, 'A one-way system was introduced on the lower corridor and a white line with arrows was painted on the floor near the walls and pupils had to walk along it. This sometimes meant that to get to an adjacent classroom a pupil had to walk the whole length of the corridor and back rather than go against the stream of traffic.' And outside the school, 'Our walking to the playing fields in Pennington and to the baths in Silk Street in crocodile is no doubt something that the older citizens of the town will remember well.'

Walking to and from that sports field is something most Old Girls will remember: the timetable rarely allowed for the length of time this took. Muriel recalls, 'The sports field was a distance away in Pennington. At least it seemed a long way then. We also had our Sports Day there. But if it was raining we danced ballroom in the Gym. I think this is where most of us learned to dance.' The parquet floor of the Gym had to be mopped by the girls before classes began and Doris remembers, 'A rigid discipline with all the gym equipment was maintained by Miss Steele, a severe Scot.' Sadie adds, 'Each lesson started with us striding around the Hall with Miss Steele chanting "Stretch your legs and cover your ground" which worked as everyone got the rhythm.' Evelyn says, 'Miss Steele didn't like me and I didn't like her. Steele by name, and steel by nature. She was very plain and masculine-looking and used to wear a hair net which came really low down on her forehead. Only two girls in our form wore glasses but that's how she referred to us – not by name but "You, the girl with the glasses on." The Gym wasn't just used for classes. Good posture was always seen as important at LGGS and the visiting nurse would often prescribe special daily exercises for any girl who showed early signs of stooping.

All girls were encouraged to take part in team sports with, it seems, limited success. The school magazine reported, 'Our hockey season has been no more successful than in previous years, although we note with some feelings of pride that the score against us was gradually lowered. Unfortunately we see no chance of great improvement until we can have more practice and more frequent matches. Owing to weather conditions, and other causes – as when one member of the team produced startling symptoms of scarlet fever and we were all contact cases – several fixtures had to be cancelled.'

The County Council promised a grant towards the cost of building a new sports pavilion down at the Pennington field, so the girls and staff started the Pavilion Fund campaign which included two performances of a staff/pupil production of *Daddy Long-legs*, a ping-pong tournament, a whist drive and sales of home-made sweets and 'dainties'. The annual Sports Day was usually held at the field in May or June so that it didn't disrupt the School Certificate and Higher School Certificate exams. Joyce remembers, 'There was a marquee on the field and teas were available. Parents were supportive but many could not afford the price of afternoon tea.'

Such costs added up, especially if you were a scholarship student. The County Scholarship included a thirty shillings book allowance and tram and train expenses, but other scholarships didn't and it wasn't easy to get one. Nora remembers, 'I was a pupil at Lowton St Luke's CE School when I passed the Junior Scholarship examination in 1937. The examination took place in the Central Council Senior School in Windermere Road. There were two arithmetic papers, an English test and an intelligence test.' Evelyn recalls, 'When I heard I'd got the Scholarship I didn't even tell my parents. It was my next door neighbours who'd heard and told them, but there was no rejoicing. My parents weren't really interested at all. They never came to the parents' evenings. When I first started I didn't even know where the school was. I'd hardly ever been to Leigh.' Sadly, winning a scholarship wasn't a guarantee you would stay for the years covered. Constance remembers, 'I won a Lancashire County Scholarship but had to leave to start work after only two years as children had no say in their careers then.' Many girls were expected to leave school early to get a job and add to the household income. At sixteen, Evelyn was told Sixth Form was out of the question as she had a job waiting for her in the offices at Bickershaw Colliery.

In 1935 a new Scholarship Fund was introduced. The anonymous benefactor offered to donate £2,000 if £500 could be raised by the school, which the girls and staff did with much enthusiasm. It was then revealed that the benefactor was Leigh's 'Fairy Godmother', Miss Marsh, only daughter of the philanthropic Marsh family, originally of Westleigh Hall. A number of girls embroidered a fire screen which was presented to Miss Marsh as a token of appreciation. The first recipient of the Miss Marsh Scholarship was Dora Wells who was studying for French Honours at the University of Manchester.

Fee-paying places were available for borderline pupils who had failed the entrance exam but whose parents wanted a better start for their daughters. However, by all accounts, these girls often found it hard to keep up with the schoolwork. Joyce vividly remembers the timetable, 'It was pinned inside your desk lid. Assembly until 9.20, two periods of thirty-five minutes until break, two periods of forty minutes after break. Lunch 12 till 1.15pm. Three periods of forty minutes in the afternoon, 1.30 till 3.30 with no break. 3.30pm pack homework and books, and change into outdoor shoes, hats and coats. 3.45pm bell for all to be out. Mistress always on cloakroom duty. Library each night from 3.30 to 4 pm supervised by prefect. No talking in the library.'

In 1932 there were three classes in each year group: *A*, *Alpha* and *Beta* or *Parallel*. This was later reduced to just *A* and *Alpha* with less able pupils placed in the *A* form where they did Domestic Science and Needlework. Doris remembers, 'We made sponges, pastry, bread, all mixed by hand, of course. Miss Bell, whose nickname was Daisy, astounded us all by deboning a chicken which still retained its shape. During our exams we happened to be the only group in school so we were allowed to choose our own menus. They were the best school dinners ever. For our cookery exam we were each given a different menu. Mine was to prepare a fowl for the oven. Thank goodness the bird was plucked and cleaned so only needed trussing.'

E. Wharton also remembers, 'In 1932 a Commercial class was introduced, where one could learn shorthand, typing and bookkeeping, taught by Mrs Collier.' For the more academic subjects, there was regular homework. Muriel remembers doing hers by oil lamp, 'Second-Formers only had two subjects per school night, each to take twenty minutes, but three subjects at weekend making one hour's study. These were increased as you rose through the school.' The homework timetable had to be signed by parents. Homework was completed in exercise books which, when full, had to be signed by the subject teacher before they could be taken to the legendary stationery office or 'Book Room'. This had been created from an old cycle house in 1924, hence its unusual location in an outside corridor. Joyce remembers, 'It only opened three days a week until 4pm when Miss Clough, helped by Amy the lab assistant, stamped each book on the last page with the school stamp. Lost books had to be paid for at sixpence a time.'

Money was also needed for school trips but it wasn't always possible to find it. Evelyn remembers, 'In the Upper Sixth we were told that we were going on a trip to Manchester by coach to see *Macbeth*. It cost 5/6- so I knew that I daren't ask my mum for the money. I wasn't the only one as four or five of us didn't go and spent the afternoon doing Maths with Miss Wareing. Fortunately, it was my favourite subject and she was a great teacher. She always taught the top set for Maths but if you'd been ill or were struggling she'd stay behind a couple of times a week to explain rather than hold the whole class up. She was very understanding. She used to say "Good morning" in German until the war started. When she was off for a term after a cycling accident, Miss Perrott's sister, a missionary, covered her classes but she couldn't teach. In fact, it may have been her who humiliated me in class. I was a nervous child who was afraid of doing anything wrong so one day when a teacher suddenly asked me about cosines in Maths and I couldn't answer she made me wear a cardboard sign with 'cosine' written on it. I was walking down the corridor when Miss Perrott stopped me and said, "Evelyn, take that off." She took it from me and must have spoken to the member of staff because it never happened again.' She also remembers a similar order from Miss Merriman, 'My older sister painted my nails one weekend and when I went into school with it still on Miss Merriman picked up my hand and said, "Take it off. Women only do that to attract attention from men.""

All the hard work of the school year was rewarded at the annual Speech or Prize Giving Day in November of the following academic year. This was held in the Co-operative Hall on Bradshawgate and all the girls had to wear white dresses for the occasion. The School Orchestra, which was a combined affair with the LGS, didn't have a great reputation, and had to be augmented by Miss Pilling, Miss Osgood, and Mr Partington of the Halle Orchestra, who was the visiting violin teacher. There was no woodwind or brass but they were conducted by Mr France, affectionately known as 'Daddy', who was apparently an erudite musician not fully appreciated by his charges. The orchestra was unable to practise until the dress rehearsal on the morning of the evening event so, unsurprisingly, had a reputation for being terrible. Mutterings of 'Oh, we're going to have a cats' chorus again' and 'Have you brought your cotton wool?' were often accompanied by a strong temptation to laugh. As attendance was compulsory, the girls had the afternoon free and a day's holiday the following day. The school song, *Land of our birth, we pledge to thee*, was sung from memory by the whole school. The governors, Mayor and Mayoress attended and sat on the platform with the Headmistress. The Chairman of Governors took charge and the Headmistress gave her report. Then the prizes, such as the John Hurst Hayes Prize, were presented by visiting notables. There were individual printed programmes for pupils and their parents, and academic regalia were worn by all staff. Joyce remembers that at the end, 'Cheers were called for. But these were said in ladylike fashion: *Hurrah* not *Hoorrray!*'

Some girls were recognised for their efforts by having their name inscribed on the Honours Board situated by the front door. This was presented to the school as a leaving present from Miss Fullerton in 1936. To be added, a girl had to attend either Oxbridge or London University. In 1939, former Head Girl (1937-38) Bessie Povah won a Major and a State Scholarship in addition to three scholarships at Manchester University. The school was given an extra day's holiday during the autumn term in honour of her success. Evelyn remembers one girl in her class who made it onto the Board despite her disability, 'Brenda Griffiths was profoundly deaf but very very clever. She used to go to somewhere in Manchester to learn how to lip read and had a hearing aid in a box that she used to place in front of her on the desk. But she didn't like French so when Miss Merriman started teaching Brenda would turn her hearing aid off, get out a book and start reading.' She won a State Scholarship, a County Scholarship and an Open Scholarship for St Hilda's College Oxford in 1945.

But school was about more than lessons. Sadie remembers, 'We spent half a day on extra-curricular subjects e.g. local government, nature walks along St Helens Road and down Beech Walk.' There were many school trips, including one to Holland which Doris remembers for the 'eighteen hours each way in a storm, which was dreadful.' They also visited the Lake District, Pennygrove, Stratford-upon-Avon, The Glasgow Exhibition and Paris. Norah remembers, 'In Easter 1937 I was privileged to join a holiday group to Paris with Miss Marlow. This holiday was for a higher form, but as there were two spare places I was able to go along with my friend, Sheila Boydell. One day we went to see some friends of Miss Marlow just outside Paris. They gave us some fruit salad but we weren't keen as they had put champagne over the fruit. We visited all the usual attractions, the Eiffel Tower, the Palace of Versailles, the Bois de Boulogne and Les Invalides where Napoleon is buried. We also saw the Venus de Milo in the Louvre, but the highlight of our trip was a visit to the Opera House. We all put our best dresses on and thought we were the belles of the ball.'

Girls were encouraged to attend the many school societies. Subs were usually 3d per term but The Guild cost sixpence for the materials needed to make items for charity such as small clothes, dolls and even dolls' beds out of chalk boxes. During this decade, the Science Society made visits to local industries such as BICC, the gasworks, Sutcliffe Speakman, and the Regal Cinema to see the projection room. The Civic Society visited the Town Hall, the fire station and new housing at Wythenshawe. The Literary Society read one-act plays and put on productions in their new Dramatic Club whilst the Craft Class tried block-printing. The school's 3rd A Leigh and 5th Leigh Guide companies had to be amalgamated as various leaders left but they still had seven patrols and 'adopted' Pendleton Guide company. The Scripture Union met on Tuesday lunchtimes, led by Miss Merriman. The school branch of the League of Nations Union held a model assembly and hosted a talk by former Mayor of Leigh, Alderman J. Ashworth, on 'How The League Prevents War'.

Sadly, war wasn't prevented so, when the air raid drills started, Evelyn remembers they had to get under their desks, 'But, of course, in the labs there were no desks, just benches, meaning there were too many girls and not enough cover. So we went part-time. Some of us went in the mornings and some of us in the afternoons until the air raid shelters were made.' These were dug, constructed and sandbagged in the playground, taking up a lot of room and restricting any outdoor games. Each girl had to carry with her at all times a warm coat, known as her 'shelter coat', and a gas mask. There were regular practices at putting them on, along with rehearsals of evacuation to the shelters. These six shelters were later adopted by the Houses and the girls planted flowers on top of them.

1939 saw the retirement of Caretaker Mr Ward after eighteen years at the school. No more would the girls be able to cry, 'My locker's stuck. Send for Ward!' or, 'This cupboard won't open. Send for Ward!' In gratitude for his faithful service, cheerful disposition and his walk-on roles in school productions, the House Captains presented him with an umbrella, a pipe and a cheque.

*

Most Talked-About Staff

Miss Dorothy Bannister BA, Maths, 1948-76
She was born in Leigh in 1918, the only child of Lewis, a policeman, and Beatrice. She attended LGGS from 1932-36 and was a member of the school magazine editorial committee, and Head Girl from 1935-36. She won a scholarship to study Mathematics at University College in London where she was awarded the Rosa Morison Medal presented to the 'most outstanding student in the year'. She initially taught in Kidderminster and Birkenhead before returning to LGGS in 1948. Described as having 'a fantastic, sharp mind', she was an excellent and very popular teacher with great enthusiasm for her subject. She was an inspiration to the girls who enjoyed Maths and very patient with those that didn't. She ran the school's Guide company with Miss Swindells. Like her famous cousin, Roger Bannister, she moved fast and is remembered as running into class with her arm outstretched, clutching a piece of chalk and talking at 100mph. In 1976 she transferred to Leigh College and, after

retiring, cared for her good friend Miss Swindells. She was devoted to maintaining the memory of LGGS. She kept all of her uniform and school books, and left a legacy to subsidise tickets for the annual Reunion Dinner. She died on 3 April 2005 and her ashes were scattered at Rivington Pike, her favourite place for walking.

Miss Dorothy J. Steele, Sport & netball team, 1926-43
She started the Sports section in the Library and donated many books and magazines. She coached hockey and the Royal Life Saving Swimming Awards, and organised Sports Days. She left LGGS to take up other work.

Miss Margaret Pilling, Biology & Music, 1928-52
From 1945, Miss Pilling was responsible for the musical life of the school, teaching Singing and Music Appreciation to the Junior and Middle Schools, and Music as an examination subject to the Fifth Form. She led the choirs, piano and recorder classes, percussion band, madrigals and orchestra, and produced music for the Christmas Concert and Music Festival. She was also House Mistress of Mackenzie.

Notable Events

On 7 May 1930 the foundation stone was laid for the new LGS building on Manchester Road, so LGGS was given a half-day holiday.

In 1931, cherry blossom trees were planted in the front garden of the school. According to Dorothy Bannister, Miss Perrott said they were planted to hide the view of the old cottages opposite.

In 1935 Jubilee Day was celebrated at the school field where there were 'run off' heats for Sports Day, and an exciting tea with cakes in red, white, and blue cases. Every girl received a Jubilee mug and medal; both these and the tea were given by Leigh Borough Council. The girls listened to King George V's speech from the Houses of Parliament, and Head Girl Dorothy Bannister planted one of several trees in Holden Road as a permanent commemoration.

The Old Girls' Association
The decade started well with an Old Girls' column in the school magazine and new Musical, Guild and Dramatic Sections introduced. But membership of the Musical and Dramatic Sections quickly dwindled so they ceased to meet. However, the Guild, hockey, netball and badminton continued. The Old Leighians of LGS proposed a joint subcommittee to organise socials but the Old Girls decided this 'wasn't wise'. However, a 'friendly relationship' continued and they took it in turns to host joint dances and a garden party with a gramophone for dancing and catering by *Millington's*. Old Girls helped out at the school Sports Day. A Benevolent Fund was introduced and members could report a needy case of any former member of LGGS. Two such Old Girls were each later awarded a grant of £10 (£711.40 today). It was decided that all past members of staff would in future be treated as Old Girls of the Association and could therefore be nominated to serve on the committee. But numbers gradually decreased so the summer meetings were discontinued.

Notable Alumni

Bessie Howarth (Head Girl LGGS 1932-33). First pupil from the school to choose a medical career as a physician and surgeon. She became a member of the National Institute of Medical Herbalists and wrote a book called *Herbal Healing Inheritance*.

Image 17

Image 18

Image 19

Image 20

The 1940s

Image 21

Headmistresses: *Miss Perrott 1927-42 / Miss Pilling (Acting Headmistress) 1939-41 / Miss Phyllis Nanney 1942-47 / Miss Shanks 1948-54*

Contributors to this chapter: *Nora Parker (née Worsley, 1937-44), G. Marsden (1939-44), Barbara Grace Wilkinson (née Hall, 1940-45), Enid Shirley Hutchinson (née Raine, 1946-51), Doreen Johnson (née Corner, 1945-52), Margaret Leigh (née Gerrard, 1945-50), Avis Freeman (née Grundy,*

1949-56), Patricia Bark (née Lane, 1948-53), Brenda M. Armitage (née Booth, 1945-52).

*

During this decade there were, technically, four different Headmistresses. As Nora remembers, 'Miss Perrott was my Headmistress for the first four years, then in her absence Miss Pilling became Acting Headmistress for the next two years, and in my final year Miss Nanney was appointed Headmistress.' She was followed by Miss Shanks. Miss Perrott had been absent for almost two years when she retired due to ill health in 1942. Miss Pilling was not one of the six candidates interviewed for the position of Headmistress but Miss Nanney, as an Oxford graduate, was clearly the best.

All four Headmistresses had to deal with problems caused by the war and its after-effects. G. Marsden remembers, 'On reflection, it is a wonderful credit to the staff that we received such a good education as we did. Lessons were often interrupted by air raid drill when we all trooped out to the shelters. But by the time everyone was accounted for and we were allowed back in the school, that particular lesson would be over.' Barbara recalls, 'Because of the ever present threat of air raids we were not allowed to use the showers. There were no swimming lessons, school visits, holidays or sports matches against other schools because of wartime travel restrictions and petrol rationing, and after-school activities were non-existent. Everyone was expected to go straight home in case of air raids.' G. Marsden adds, 'There were no school photographs as films were in short supply but we did have lunchtime concerts with quite well-known artists. One I will never forget. Astra Desmond was booked to sing but had to cancel at the last moment so we were sent a newcomer by the name of Kathleen Ferrier – need I say more?' The singer went on to achieve an international reputation as a stage, concert and recording artist.

In 1940 the British government introduced food rationing which affected Cookery lessons but also school dinners. Barbara recalls, 'Meals were rather frugal. The main course was a portion of fish or meat with boiled potatoes and one vegetable, usually carrots or peas. The second course was a portion of milk or steamed sponge pudding or jelly. The jelly was usually diluted to go round and semi-solid which made it difficult to eat with a fork.' Enid adds, 'School dinners in the Hall cost two shillings per week paid to the Secretary Miss Bent on Friday mornings before 9am. I have memories of cheese pie, liver and bacon, potatoes, minced meat and gravy topped with pickled beets, toad-in-the-hole, tureens of mashed potatoes and gravy boats, semolina pudding in vanilla or chocolate, and currants in pastry – the famous LGGS "fly pie" – with custard.' The white, gravy-stained, tablecloths were replaced with chequered oilcloth in green, red, blue and yellow which Miss Swindells was later to describe as 'a rather horrible linoleum' when she joined the school in 1946, adding, 'A new Kitchen and Dining Room in 1948 altered our life in many ways. Perhaps [what] the staff will remember clearly and rather sadly was that High Tea of sandwiches and cake at 3.30pm was no longer served in the Staffroom.' Doreen remembers the staff having to go across to the Dining Room for coffee, 'Perhaps there was no water supply in the Staffroom at that time. Miss Seacombe, who was always so thin, used to wrap herself up in her gown to go across the cold playground.'

The new Dining Room/Kitchen unit, built at the Tax Office end of the school yard, meant the girls no longer had to help to set up the trestle tables for lunch, but there was some disappointment that it closed the 'short cut' across the playground. Along the Walmesley Road boundary there were a few scrubby hawthorn trees with openings in them which were a convenient way of entering and leaving school via 'the hole in the hedge'.

In 1941 clothing coupons were introduced so uniform regulations had to be relaxed slightly. Panama hats were no longer regulatory and there was no school summer dress. Brenda's mother had wanted to stay on at school herself, 'but her family couldn't afford the costs involved. She went to work at fourteen as a seamstress and became very skilled. Her great wish was that her two daughters should have the opportunity she had been denied. She made our school uniforms: blouses, gym slips, and gabardines. They matched perfectly the expensive items which were supposed to be bought from the school outfitter in Leigh.' In Needlework the teachers had to make do with what they could get which, according to Margaret, must have been easy for Miss Bell as she always wore the same autumn-coloured tweed outfit which she claimed to have collected, spun, dyed and woven the wool for. But Margaret and her friends were in hysterics over the fabric they were given to make knickers from, 'It was a pale blue rough cotton that was just short of being denim. I should have kept them because they were hilarious. We had to make our own pattern to our own measurements. We had to put our foot on a stool so that someone else could measure from the waist down to the back of the knee. They had a double crotch, too. Real passion killers. But I did go on to make a lot of my own clothes and some for my children, so something must have stuck.'

Margaret remembers a shortage of paper meant they often had to write between the lines in their exercise books. As a result, the school magazine was reduced to one issue per year but, in 1943, it reported 'A number of changes in school regulations have given us a greater measure of freedom in school, and it is up to all to show our appreciation by the development of a fuller sense of responsibility.' The girls certainly had to do this when a severe shortage of room meant some forms had to move into the old Primitive Methodist School. Miss Swindells remembers that in 1947, with 487 on the roll, 'Three new Second Forms had arrived in the Sunday School and two of them had to make the twice-daily journey to school and face a bewildering search for classrooms whose simple scheme of numbering they seemed quite unable to grasp. After a month, the building outlook was judged to be distinctly gloomy; the Lower Sixth took up residence in the Cookery Room, struggling nobly with their books in the one-time Upper Sixth cloakroom, one of the Thirds migrated to the Dining Room and we gave IIB and IIS classrooms on the premises. Music classes continued to run to and fro the Sunday School where Miss Pilling, exiled without her treasured Bechstein piano, the radiogram and most of her equipment, cheerfully contrived to prove that delight in music can triumph over many difficulties.' A new 'hut' or 'prefab classroom' had been promised but, 'Our interest in the Hut waxed and waned throughout the winter and we could scarcely believe our good fortune at the beginning of the Summer Term when everything was ready at last and Upper Sixth Classics and Third Classics were selected as the first tenants. They moved in joyfully, really thrilled by the light and airy rooms – the blue paint, the new desks and the delightful sensations of being "on our own". Their good spirits do not appear to have been daunted by much subsequent running to and fro in mackintoshes.' This HORSA or 'Hutting Operation for the Raising of the School-Leaving Age' hut was the one nearest to the main building, into which the Library would later move.(*continues on p81*)

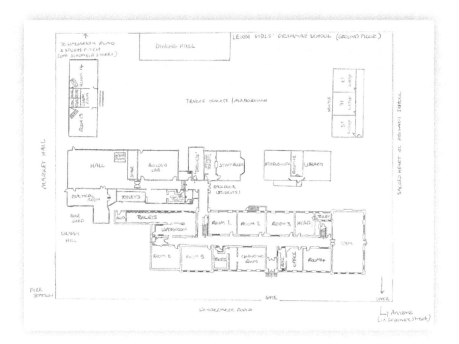

Image 41

Image 42

77

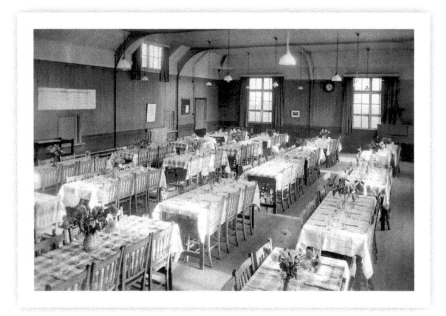

Image 43

Image 44

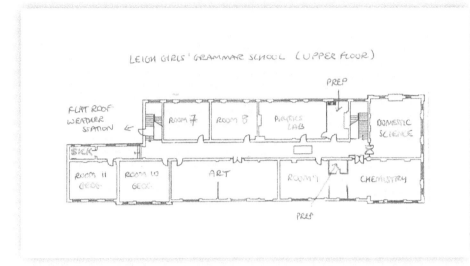

Image 45

Image 46

Image 47

Image 48

(continued from p75). At her interview for the post of Science mistress, apologies were made to Miss Swindells for the rather dated design of the Chemistry lab and, 'I was assured of two improvements – immediately a new Science block was to be built on the playground with the Chemistry lab upstairs. And it was pointed out to me the great advantage of being able to see any visitors approaching across the playground. But, much more important, a new school was to be begun any day on the playing fields at Pennington [...]. We have always been a "wandering school" and when the governors questioned the safety of girls who had to use the C.E. Infant School in Union Street and thereby cross Leigh Road, Lancashire County showed little concern and said our girls were accustomed to walking through the town. And indeed I always regarded this as a safety valve for the school and a good thing that girls could walk through the town with the townspeople and very few complaints.'

Of course the new building never materialised. Miss Swindells had a theory about this, 'I think we probably kept the front of the school, the entrance hall and the bottom corridor, too well so that anyone coming in got the wrong impression.'

The impression of many people today is that grammar schools were only for those who could afford to pay, but the number of 'free places' at LGGS had been steadily increasing since it opened. In 1944 the introduction of the 'Butler' Education Act meant any girl could now be offered a place if she passed the 11+ exam and could stay on in education up to age eighteen and beyond. Aimed at removing inequalities in secondary education, the new Act forbade fee-paying at state schools and the school leaving age was raised to fifteen. Although the intention was to open up grammar schools to pupils from working-class backgrounds, many parents were unhappy with the new leaving age as it delayed their children adding to the family income. The uniform also continued to be a financial barrier. Margaret remembers, 'My father only had a menial job and didn't earn a big wage, so we got National Assistance. I got some money towards my uniform and had free school dinners but there wasn't any money for extras. I remember once needing white knickers for a play and I didn't have any. That was so embarrassing. In the Fifth Form they pushed you to stay on but my father was fifty when I was born so he needed me to go to work. Parents were different in those days – you did as you were told.' Doreen recalls, 'It was my ambition to go to Oxford or Cambridge but, in the event, I left school at fifteen. I was the eldest of five children so it was decided that it was too expensive for me to go to Sixth Form. However, when I got a good School Certificate, Miss Shanks wrote to my father and he agreed that I could go back. But it was hard work so I never got to Oxford except for an interview for a Miners' Welfare Scholarship. I wanted to do medicine but that was a five- or six-year degree course which was also expensive so in the end I went to Nottingham and read Pharmacy.'

Doreen was in the second year group to take the 11+ exam. 'I'd no idea what I was doing. It was just another test to me. I think we went to Leigh Central to do it.' Avis recalls, 'It was just an exam, the whole class took it at Lowton County Primary. But it was done on a Saturday morning and there were three parts: English, Comprehension and Maths.' Patricia remembers, 'Two other girls and myself who were going to go to LGGS had to be interviewed by Miss Shanks because our eleventh birthdays were not until after the start of the school term. I don't know on what basis we were assessed but we were all allowed to start in September 1948 aged ten.' Passing the 11+, or the previous entrance exam, was just the first challenge as Margaret recalls, 'You realised when you got to Grammar School that you weren't quite as clever as you thought you were. You went from a big fish in a small pond to a little fish in a big pond. I'd been top of my class all through junior school but suddenly found myself amongst much cleverer girls.' But the streaming system was designed to get the best out of each girl and, although the names changed over time, the principle stayed the same. Margaret again, 'After the seconds, we were grouped into Classics (Latin), Modern (Language) or Science (Two Sciences).' Brenda recalls, 'There was no explanation given of how or why girls had been sorted into one of the three forms.'

Doreen and Avis were both put into the Science stream in their respective years, and both became members of the renamed Scientific Society which met after school. This was organised by the girls, with the guidance of staff, and arranged visiting lecturers, trips to coal mines and other local industries, and a quiz in 1949 in which they beat the LGS boys 37-34. 'We also used to clean the apparatus in the Chemistry lab, polish the brass taps and wash the glassware, always remembering to rinse three times.' Clearly the girls were expected to contribute more to the upkeep of the building in those days as the Library was closed for several weeks while the Lower Sixth carried out spring-cleaning operations. They also re-catalogued the books according to the Dewey system. That sense of duty and responsibility was no doubt reinforced in a careers talk by a representative from the Women's Employment Federation, an organisation concerned with the employment and training of educated women, and certainly in LGGS' many clubs and societies. As G. Marsden recalls, 'We were taught about much more than the subjects listed on the school curriculum: good manners, team spirit and a sense of our own worth.'

The School Guild and Guild of Service were superseded by The Ship Adoption Society which sent letters and parcels of gifts made by members to the officers and crews of *M.V. Artist, S.S. Ramava* and the *S.S. Bercleuch*. Meanwhile, the Appeals Fund sent subscriptions to various charities and there was a competition to raise funds for the Red Cross, which involved recognising flags, service badges and aircraft. Prizes included pen-knives and pocket dominoes. Other societies supported the curriculum by developing a wider body of knowledge. The Classics Society hosted visiting lecturers giving lantern slide talks such as 'Women in Ancient Athens'. The Discussion Group, led by Miss Seacombe, discussed many controversial topics including 'Notoriety is a preferable state to nonentity'. Miss Seacombe was to become notorious herself, remembered by some old girls more for her appearance than for her teaching skills. As Margaret recalls, 'We had her for History. We used to think that she'd dipped her face in the flour bag because she was always so white. I don't know what she put on her face. All she seemed to do was to write notes on the board. She gave very few verbal lectures. I learned more about history after I left school.' But others, like Doreen, found her inspiring because of her Oxford degree and her obvious intellect. Like most of the staff, Miss Seacombe certainly appears to have enjoyed supporting, encouraging and challenging the girls outside her classes.

The Literary Society, which had become the Junior and Senior Dramatic Societies, continued to put on productions of Shakespeare and modern plays. Music groups, including a Madrigal Society, Recorder Group and Junior and Senior Choirs, took part in the annual Music Festival. There were also puppet clubs, cycling clubs, and an art group whose members embroidered a curtain for the entrance hall. The 3rd Leigh Guide Company took part in a Thinking Day ceremony in which they remembered Guides in other countries. Meanwhile, a German girl visited the school, studying for a term in the Upper Sixth Modern, and girls were encouraged to write to pen friends all around the world. The Junior Film Society was thrilled by *The 39 Steps*, and the newly formed Senior Film Society watched a film about Radar and several foreign films.

Following the end of the war in 1945, school holidays resumed with trips to Stratford-upon-Avon, Derbyshire, Switzerland and Paris, and one to Sweden with boys and staff from LGS. Patricia remembers, 'In 1948 some of the Seconds went to Whiteacre Camp School in Barrow for a couple of weeks. The accommodation was in long single-storey buildings and was quite spartan. The food was very poor and I remember parents coming on visiting day loaded with food parcels.' Staff gave up their free time to accompany and supervise the girls on holidays, and at weekends for sports fixtures when the hockey team made up for their lack of success with their enthusiasm. The netball, tennis and rounders teams fared slightly better but, generally, it was felt the secret to their success would lie in more constant and conscientious practice. Perhaps they could have learned from members of the Folk Dance Society, led by Miss Hersee, who, in addition to their regular sessions, went to Manchester to attend courses in morris-, sword- and country-dancing. Few girls would have realised activities were supported by staff who boarded in Leigh during the week, only going home at weekends. Avis remembers that, for some time, 'Miss Seacombe, who was from Radcliffe near Bolton, resided from Monday to Friday in "rooms" with a family in Pennington. Miss Norminton, who lived in Stockport, and Miss Swindells, who was from Oldham, both stayed in houses over Pennington Bridge, too.'

Although Miss Nanney was born only twenty-five miles away in Wilmslow, she was apparently so appalled by the local accent that she insisted on elocution tuition being given at every assembly, led by Miss Hyatt. Barbara remembers, 'Each morning the whole assembly had to do speech exercises and end by chanting one of several rhymes, e.g. *Peter Piper picked a peck of pickled peppers.*' Miss Nanney may have been behind the introduction of the Posture Stripe, a red strip of ribbon, which encouraged good deportment around the school. In her five years as Headmistress she must have made many small changes, but one provoked a rare rebellion in 1944. As G. Marsden recalls, 'This particular School Leaving was memorable for the fact that it was the only occasion when the whole school, with the connivance of Mr Burkhill, dared to defy Miss Nanney. We had always marched out to the tune of *Country Gardens* but on this particular occasion, she had decreed that we should have something more classical and stately. We pleaded to keep "our" marching-out music but to no avail. Mr Burkhill said, "Leave it to me". We heard nothing more so gave up hope. But that day, as we stood to march out, the school orchestra started to play *Country Gardens*. Miss Nanney's face was a study but, fortunately, Mr Burkhill just happened to be leaving the same day to take up another appointment.' Mr Burkhill was one of very few male teachers in the school at that time. Avis and Doreen don't remember any except for the Reverend who came in to teach RE.

School Leaving was one of several key events in the calendar along with Remembrance Day, when the school attended the service at the War Memorial, and Founder's or Commemoration Day, held in November every year at the Parish Church. It appears the service rarely changed as several old girls from different years remember the opening hymn *Now Thank We All Our God* and the set prayers and readings. A less formal annual event was the School Christmas Party for which, Doreen remembers, 'My mother bought me some lipstick. I was fifteen.' The food was limited because of rationing, as Avis recalls, 'You would only have two small sandwiches made from one slice of bread, and a jelly and a small cake' but, from 1950 onwards, the party was enhanced by Miss Wareing's leaving gift of an annual Christmas tree.

In 1944, there was a growing feeling that the Form was a more natural unit than the House which led to a discussion between representatives of the Houses and the staff, and finally to the girls voting for the system they preferred. As a result, the House system was suspended with the focus placed on Form-based activities including the termly election of Form Captain. But, due to wartime shortages, the customary metal badge had to be replaced with one of printed cloth.

Prize Giving was still held at the Co-operative Hall, but in 1947, owing to the enormous number of pupils, they had to restrict the number of parents attending. Some prizes were awarded in honour of former members of staff, such as the Miss Elsie G. Beddow Classics Prize and the Miss Fullerton Progress Prize. Doreen remembers, 'I won my first Form Prize for Science. This was awarded for getting the highest average mark across all the forms. I was always thrilled to bits. You were told in advance that you'd won so you could choose a book as your prize. I remember one year I asked for a book about Apartheid in South Africa. They weren't sure at first but eventually agreed. They were all beautiful hardback books embossed with LGGS and I still won't part with them.' Avis remembers winning a Geography prize and believes such rewards encouraged girls to do their best.

The arrival of Miss Shanks in 1948 brought change as *A, Alpha* and *Beta* or *Parallel* were replaced with 2X, 2Y, 2Z for the Seconds, and the uniform was updated. The old-fashioned pleated gym slip was replaced with a V-necked tunic with a flared skirt, worn with a white, collared blouse and school tie and girdle. There was also an optional metal *Swift and Sure* badge. Gloves were no longer compulsory but the school hat still was. Patricia remembers, 'The velour hats were smaller and darker than the felt ones and more expensive. There was a certain snob value in owning one and, I am ashamed to say, we used to judge whether or not other pupils' families were well off according to the type of hat they wore.' Navy blue socks could be worn instead of stockings and were replaced with white socks in the summer. The summer dress returned in plain blue, the material for which was available from *Danby's* and could be made up into any style within reason. Shoes could be black or brown. Smart white dresses were worn for tennis, and navy blue culottes were now allowed for sport, but the 1949 school magazine ends with a photograph of the Netball Team all posing happily for the photographer, still in their blouses and knickers.

*

Most Talked-About Staff

Miss Mary Bent, School Secretary & Bursar, 1948-72
She used to travel to school on her bike and was always cheerful and helpful to girls and staff alike. She was famous for her kindness, tact and efficiency, dealing with all admin and transport arrangements. She was Chairman of the School Secretaries' Association from 1963-64.

Miss Beatrice Norma Seacombe MA, History, 1947-76
Born 20 November 1923 in Bolton, she studied History at Oxford. She used to catch two buses from Radcliffe to Leigh and back every day, taking the opportunity to read *Le Figaro*. She always wore her academic gown, serious and austere-looking, but in reality was shy and introverted. When LGGS closed she joined Leigh College. She died in Fairfield Hospital, Bury, on 28 March 2004. The books found at her bedside were the *Oxford Book of 16th Century Verse*, Rowan Williams' *Anglican Identities* and a little book of cat pictures.

Miss Winifred Hersee, French & German, 1943-52
She took a year out to work in Vienna where she taught square-dancing. She led the Folk Dance Society country-dancing classes and recorder class, and made costumes for school productions. She arranged regular exchange visits with German pupils and took school parties to Germany, France and Austria. She married after leaving LGGS and continued her teaching career in London.

Notable Events

In December 1947, Miss Marsh died. She was a School Governor and had created the Miss Marsh Scholarship.

In October 1948, the 5th Music Festival was held, the adjudicator being Miss Helen Henschel, a well known music broadcaster from BBC *Children's Hour*.

In 1949, at the birthday celebrations in school, a lecture on 'The Appreciation of Architecture' was given to the Seniors while the Juniors were entertained by Captain Knight and his golden eagle.

The Old Girls' Association

The contents of the Benevolent Fund were transferred to the Trustee Savings Bank to earn interest and £10 was invested in Defence Bonds. Old Girls were asked to volunteer to help out with the fire-watching of the school. The Secretary/Treasurer joined the Auxiliary Services and was given an honorarium of one guinea as a token of appreciation. It was agreed that all Old Girls serving with the forces should have their subscriptions suspended for the duration of the war, and that the Benevolent Fund be used for training as well as sickness. The Dramatic Society was restarted along with a Music group and a Keep Fit class, all meeting fortnightly, but these were soon abandoned as more and more Old Girls found war work. However, a second annual meeting was reintroduced. Whist Drives remained one of the most popular activities and, at the Christmas party, games were popular, including egg cup and balls, indoor hockey, nursery rhymes, musical arms and musical chairs. After the war ended, a joint dramatics society with the Old Leighians was proposed but it was stressed that 'equal representation should be insisted upon'. This was extended to sketching, rambling, badminton, table tennis, an orchestra and two American tournaments of tennis, round-robin-style mixed doubles competitions.

Notable Alumni

Lynda Lee Potter (née Higginson) OBE (1935-2004). Author, journalist and columnist for the *Daily Mail*. 'First Lady of Fleet Street', British Woman Writer of the Year Award 1989, winner of the Columnist of the Year Award twice.

Image 22

Image 23

Image 24

Image 25

The 1950s

Image 26

Headmistresses: *Miss Shanks 1948-54 / Miss Hulme 1954-61*

Contributors to this chapter: *Doreen Johnson (née Corner, 1945-52), Brenda M. Armitage (née Booth, 1945-52), Patricia Bark (née Lane, 1948-53), Avis Freeman (née Grundy, 1949-56), Jean Williamson (née Hilton, 1954-59), Janet Mary Mann (née Taylor, 1955-62), Margaret Leigh* *(née Gerrard, 1945-50), Vivien J. Davies (née Jones, 1952-9), Jean Woodward (née Whittaker, 1950-7).*

*

In May 1951 eleven of the Lower Sixth girls went to the Festival of Britain in London which celebrated the country's achievements and encouraged the public to be optimistic about the future following the devastation of war. Doreen recalls, 'We stayed in a deep shelter which had been built during the war under the Underground. It was quite frightening but we had a rare old time.' The girls and their teachers had to descend 120 feet by lift to sleep in the two-tiered beds of the Deep Shelter in Clapham South.

Later that year, in November, the school had a celebration of its own for its thirtieth anniversary. Brenda remembers, 'A service took place in the Parish Church. The hymns, prayers and readings made it a very solemn event. We had to behave perfectly, even if we weren't directly involved and didn't understand the procedures or even much of the language used. The closing prayer had more relevance for me, as it was for the life of the school and all those with positions of responsibility, including "prefects of the school" and finally "all the pupils".'

Most of the pupils were now facing a big change as the School Certificate was abolished and the GCE O-Levels introduced. Patricia remembers, 'Before going into the Upper Sixth we had to choose between Art, Music, RE, Physics, Biology or Domestic Science. This subject would then be studied up to O-Level and taken in addition to Maths, French, English Language, English Literature, History, Geography, and Latin, German or Chemistry. In the Lower School, everyone did some Needlework, but Cookery was not available until Miss Hill arrived at the school to replace Miss Bell. She was a young enthusiastic teacher and she was very pleased when she was able to offer Domestic Science at O-Level. Our year was the first to have this option.'

Despite this new option, the main focus of the school's curriculum was still fiercely academic and girls were encouraged to think for themselves. In 1951, the Labour government called a snap election in the hope of increasing its parliamentary majority and the school organised its own mock version to give the girls an insight into politics. Apparently, the walls of the corridors and form rooms were covered with posters; regular meetings attracted enthusiastic crowds and at the eve-of-poll meeting both candidates addressed the school appealing for votes. The Conservative candidate won with 170 votes to 123 for Labour. An enjoyable exercise with a serious underlying message at a time when there were only seventeen female MPs, a meagre 2.7% of the total elected.

There was another important national event in 1953 with the Coronation of Queen Elizabeth II. The school magazine reports, 'The outstanding feature of the School year has undoubtedly been the Coronation. The spirit of this event has permeated the normal School atmosphere and produced one of festivity and patriotism. The School garden is now gay with red, white and blue flowers, and as June 2nd approached many of the Junior Form rooms sported decorations and photographs of the Royal Family.' A Coronation Ball was held in Leigh Church Institute for the Fifth and Sixth Forms, whilst the other forms had parties in the school Hall. A Coronation souvenir was presented to each member of the school and, as a permanent commemorative gift, a notice-board was erected at the front of the building. However, the magazine states, 'The Coronation overshadowed the more serious topic of examinations and the fact that the school buildings are slowly sinking into subterranean regions. Doors have stubbornly refused to shut and plaster has cracked or been removed to allow brickwork to be inspected.'

In 1952, the L-shaped Practical Room or 'Impractical Room', as Avis called it, had been added to the Hall and the whole school was redecorated. But space was still at a premium and the Primitive Methodist School was joined by the cold, draughty Old Vicarage as an overspill space for the smaller Sixth Form classes. A surge in births after World War Two resulted in 'bulge' years in the 1950s. These were additional classes added to accommodate the rising enrolment at the school. Jean remembers, '1954 must have been a bulge year because there were four Seconds instead of the usual three. I was in Form 2S. We took the initial of our form mistress, Miss Smale. There were thirty-six of us and our form room that year was the small hall of the Primitive Chapel, opposite the fire station. Whenever the fire siren went off the sound nearly deafened us and, if we were in the middle of a lesson, whoever was taking it had to stop because they couldn't be heard. But if we were between lessons awaiting a member of staff and the siren went off, we would race to the gate and watch the fire crews as they hastily donned their jackets and helmets and got into the fire engine. The novelty soon wore off. We quickly discovered that the Chapel had a larger hall, complete with stage, next door to our smaller hall. It was really out of bounds, but whilst waiting for members of staff to come over from school, we held our own impromptu concerts there. I think we all quite enjoyed the independence of being away from the main school but it must have been a bother to the staff during the winter months having to put on coats and get umbrellas just to come over to take a lesson. It was equally frustrating for us having nowhere to hang our clothes in school. We ended up carrying our satchels and PE bags around with us and dumping everything else in the showers in a great pile.'

Other girls at the school did at least have somewhere to store their belongings. As Patricia remembers, 'We had a different form room each year and this is where we stored our books. Whichever desk you chose at the beginning of the school year was yours for the whole three terms. I remember my friend and I getting a very early bus on the first day of the school year so that we would have a good choice of desks. The lift-up lids always had a copy of the timetable stuck on the inside. Four lessons in the morning with a break in the middle, three lessons in the afternoon and school finishing at 3.30pm. The desks were not locked and books were taken out for the morning lessons and changed at lunchtime. The only books taken home were the ones needed for homework.' As Janet says, 'There was no stealing of books. I don't even remember anyone losing one. We backed our exercise books with wallpaper each September. We went to the stationery cupboard to get new ones. Oh, the lovely smell of the place.'

Patricia remembers other essential school equipment, 'We had to use fountain pens as Biros were forbidden, and most girls had an impressive array of pencils of varying degrees of hardness, coloured pencil crayons, compasses, set square, protractor, ruler and the essential rubber. Leather satchels were the norm with two buckles to fasten them and a long strap.' The compass, of course, was essential for scratching your name on the inside of your desk lid. These were the original double desks on a metal frame with holes for ink wells and bench seats that you had to slide into.

The satchel was part of the school uniform, which remained the same for this decade, except for the addition of an optional Aertex blouse for Gym and the first mention of a red and navy blue striped wool scarf. Patricia also remembers owning, 'a hockey stick, boots and shin pads, but these were optional. It was very unfortunate the school was situated in the middle of town without a nearby playing field. It seemed a long walk down to the games field and even longer to Pennington Park for tennis in the summer. There didn't seem to be much time for actual games by the time everyone had made their way down.' Some girls dreaded sport. As one old girl comments, 'I hated running round the field twice in blouse and knickers, then getting my ankles pelted with a hockey ball.' But for others, like Brenda, 'Team sport was very important to me, particularly hockey. I was Team Captain. We travelled by public bus to play matches against other schools as far away as Saint Helens and Rivington. It meant being with friends and learning to accept that we couldn't win every time. We were ambassadors for our school and we learned to be good hosts to visiting teams.'

Girls were encouraged to behave appropriately at all times. Although there were no Houses, Patricia remembers, 'Good and bad marks were given and each form had a chart on the wall to record those awarded to each member. At the end of the year the winning form was given a print of the *Mona Lisa* to put on their form room wall. We had examinations at the end of each term and termly reports which were quite elaborate with the Tree of Knowledge printed on the front, along with the name of the school and the term. An average mark for the term's work was given for each subject, and a percentage, together with the place in the form, for the examination in that subject. Remarks from each Subject Teacher and a summary were signed by the Form Teacher and the Headmistress. There was also the age of the pupil, the average age of the form, and the number of times late.'

Lateness, along with absences, would be noted and questioned. Patricia again, 'It was a well disciplined existence. We knew exactly what we could and could not do and what the consequences would be if we broke the rules. I remember the settle near the front door, a door never used by pupils, and the Headmistress' office. Anyone seen sitting on it was assumed to be waiting for punishment and was the object of everyone's attention as we walked past to change rooms during lessons.' Another old girl recalls, 'I remember the dreaded words "Go and sit on the settle." This always meant detention. I got a week's detention once and dreaded telling my mother. However, she happened to be working late that week so I kept silent. The only problem was that within two weeks there was a Parents' at Home and Miss Shanks apologised to my mother for keeping me late at school. I got hell when we got home.'

Vivien remembers the formality of behaviour in school, 'In class, the door monitor would be waiting for the teacher and then we heard a whispered, "She's coming!" At this we all stood to attention like soldiers on parade in hushed silence waiting for the "Good morning, girls" before sitting down. If another member of staff entered during the lesson we would be up and down like yo-yos. If a member of staff, particularly Mrs Pennycuick, approached a door a girl was expected to dash in front and hold it open. The staff members were set apart from the girls and the Staffroom was totally out of bounds, a holy of holies. The only way to ever see inside was to return as a teacher.' Mrs Pennycuick was to become the school's first Deputy Head, a new post demanded under Local Education Authority rules due to the increased number of pupils.

To help maintain good order, selected girls were promoted to the position of prefect, a system introduced when the school first opened. Brenda says, 'I saw the Senior girls and prefects, who were clearly important, so confident, so much older. They had responsibilities. They wore badges of "office". They were role models. So when I joined the Sixth Form I was pleased to be made a prefect.' Vivien remembers, 'As a prefect, there was "door duty" to stop any Juniors sneaking in out of the cold, making sure all hats were on heads on the journey home, and heaven forbid anyone should be caught eating anything. Silence was the rule en route to assembly and anyone caught speaking could land in prefect's detention. The most important thing was to become a prefect and wear a badge on your tie or become the Deputy or Head Girl.'

Brenda did become Head Girl in September 1954, 'It was a huge honour. Selection for this prestigious role was made by the teachers, with the Headmistress playing an important part. I led the prefects and listened to suggestions from Senior pupils. In a school of over 500 girls, there were many issues, talking points and suggestions, some of which could improve the wellbeing of the girls and thus benefit the school. I could raise concerns with members of staff where appropriate and I had access to Miss Shanks. I could talk to her about general matters of concern raised by the prefects and Seniors, as well as developing my own views and opinions. I represented the school on important occasions, welcoming visitors and escorting them round the school, and greeting outside speakers who had come to give talks to the various societies. Giving the Vote of Thanks to the main guests at Prize Day, in a full Co-operative Hall, was the most public and nerve-racking occasion. On the platform with Miss Shanks were the school governors, the Mayor, and usually a distinguished academic or church leader who would present the prizes and make a speech designed to recognise and encourage achievement and service to others in the future. Our teachers looked most impressive; they were dressed for the occasion in their academic gowns and silk hoods in various bright colours. I had always wanted to be a teacher but neither I nor my family knew anything about university. They just believed that a good education was the way to a better life than they had. I can't remember who explained the system to me but I knew what I had to aim for.'

Miss Shanks herself was aiming for promotion and left in 1954 to become Headmistress of The Park School, Preston. Miss Swindells was interviewed to become the next Headmistress but the position went to Miss Hulme who inherited all the accommodation problems at the school.

Although the Sixth Form's classrooms in the Old Vicarage weren't ideal they did at least have some special privileges, as Vivien remembers, 'They had a bright red tie, and skirts instead of tunics. Their cloakroom was actually heated which made a pleasant change from the frozen line of Junior toilets.' They also had dances with the boys of LGS. As Doreen recalls, 'We had a party at the boys' school that was due to finish at 9.30pm. We were all dancing away when Mr Major suddenly stopped the music and said, 'It's 9.30pm.' He was a Quaker so he probably didn't approve.' Avis adds, 'We had a Sixth Form dance with LGS too but it was very artificial because unless you had a brother there, or someone you knew at primary school, you wouldn't really know any of them. So the boys tended to sit on one side and the girls on the other.' Perhaps this is why the Folk Dance Society later introduced American square-dancing into the Sixth Form party.

The Folk Dance Society also introduced Scottish dancing to their repertoire, and barn dances and, despite losing their founder Miss Hersee, continued to be popular. Music continued to thrive with the orchestra, madrigal and recorder groups and Senior and Junior choirs. Miss Shanks introduced the annual Carol Service, and the school bought season tickets for three Sixth-Formers to attend mid-week Hallé Orchestra concerts, encouraging a lifelong appreciation of classical music. Meanwhile, the Classical Society had guest lectures such as 'Aqueducts and Drains in Ancient Rome', regularly visited Chester and York, and enjoyed reading plays, inspiring a Fourth Form performance of the Nativity in Latin. The Discussion Group, led throughout by Miss Seacombe, enjoyed numerous 'balloon' debates in which members had to decide who, from a selection of important historical figures, should survive a fatal crash. They also debated more serious topics, including 'Spare the rod and spoil the child', but numbers dwindled and by 1959 the group had folded. The Film Society also faded away this decade despite its obvious popularity. A Senior and a Junior section had been formed to accommodate the 250 members who were watching three films a term but, with seven cinemas in Leigh to choose from at the time, perhaps the girls just preferred to watch films in more comfort. The Drama Group maintained both Senior and Junior groups. In 1952, the Seniors were rehearsing *The Tempest* and the school magazine describes Miss Bannister as 'the most efficient business manager, while Doreen Corner (the future Mrs Johnson) and her helpers could be relied upon to keep everything under control behind the scenes'. The following year, the producers and most of the cast had flu and, unable to hire their usual stage swords, they apparently ended up performing their duel scenes wielding enormous rapiers and missing each other by inches. The Juniors worked on their elocution and speech-making and both groups entered Speech and Drama Festivals with some success. In 1958 the Literary Society, which was formed in 1924 and later became the Drama Group, was revived by Miss Hughes and focused on reading prose, plays and poetry. From 1959, Russian was offered, as an experiment, with the Reverend Cowling whose good looks apparently added to its appeal.

The Library continued to encourage girls to read more widely. The member of staff in charge, Miss Smale from 1956, was assisted by a Library Committee of Sixth- and Fifth-Formers which organised various activities such as publicity and the collection of library money. To commemorate the Coronation, each form collected money to buy a book that it presented to the Library. In 1958, the Library was redecorated in pastel grey and blue with a pink ceiling, and the Seconds' Library was moved to Room 9. The Scientific Society started a new Junior section and later introduced a Naturalist Group, a Natural History Section and a Laboratory Group which met in the Chemistry laboratory. According to Avis, who was then the Secretary, 'as yet they have not succeeded in blowing the school up'. There was also a Scientific Meeting organised by Miss Swindells at which there were various experiments and demonstrations by girls from the Upper Fourth, Fifth and Sixth Forms. Although the Third Leigh Guide Company started the decade strongly with beetle drives, rambles and cook-outs, by 1959 they were no longer mentioned. A branch of the Student Christian Movement was introduced, replacing the Scripture Union which had disappeared in the 1940s, and there was also a new Craft Class and Modern Languages Society.

Sport continued to play a large part in school life. Although matches were regularly cancelled due to bad weather, the netball, hockey and rounders teams were increasingly competitive and successful, taking part in local and regional competitions including the Lancashire Schools Rally at Preston. But Jean remembers, 'We were the only school at inter-school matches wearing knickers as the chief item of apparel. Plus the sight of seventeen- and eighteen-year-old girls playing netball every lunchtime always attracted loads of men outside the fencing by the Dining Room.'

There were regular tennis and gymnastic tournaments and, in 1957, three girls represented LGGS at the Lancashire Schools Athletics Championships held at White City Stadium in Manchester. An after-school swimming period was secured at Leigh Baths to allow time for extra training and, as a result, the school won the Leigh Schools Swimming Cup for the first time. There were lots of school trips and holidays including a pen friend exchange in Hamburg, a marine biology field excursion to Robin Hood's Bay, youth-hostelling in the Lake District and Stratford-upon-Avon, skiing trips to Switzerland, and even a holiday in Norway.

But none of this was allowed to distract from the serious business of school and, crucially, what a girl would do after school. There were regular careers talks including a lecture by Miss Higginson, Headmistress of Manchester Road Secondary Modern School, in which she explained the difficulties of teaching in a secondary modern school, and gave helpful advice to those contemplating a teaching career. Brenda remembers, 'I had found out that to teach in a grammar school I needed a university degree. Miss Norminton, my geography teacher, was a Manchester graduate and wore the beautiful blue silk hood with white fur at the annual Prize Day celebration. At Liverpool University, A. J. Monkhouse was a lecturer who had written a book on Physical Geography which I received as a school prize and loved. On such a naïve basis I decided to apply to each. I have no memory of how I did this – was it a handwritten letter? Did I have a prospectus? Did Miss Norminton, or any other teacher, give advice? Not that I can remember. Miss Shanks did write supporting letters on my behalf and I chose to go to Manchester University. I became a Geography teacher at Levenshulme High School for Girls in 1959. My head of department at the school was Miss Bessie Povah, who, to my surprise, had been Head Girl at LGGS in 1937-38 and was a Geography graduate of Manchester University.'

Doreen did her degree and returned to LGGS as a teacher in 1958, 'One of the staff was being whipped off to India with her husband so there was a knock at the front door and Miss Bent said, "I wonder if you could do a bit of part-time teaching for me?" Because it was Science, you only needed a degree as a qualification.' There were already several old girls on the staff who had also enjoyed their time at LGGS. As Patricia remembers, 'The school was small enough to know every face, though not every name of the pupils, and we knew the names of all the staff.' Janet loved 'the orderliness and the friendships and stimulus of the subjects studied. A girls' school suited me as it protected me while I grew up. I loved the personalities, the rituals and the seasonal events.' Vivien states, 'In July 1959 I was not ready to leave this place that had been home for seven years. Our teachers were devoted to our needs and really wanted us to be successful in our careers. A sense of belonging was good for us and we made strong friendships. I am glad I had LGGS in my formative years and will never forget the great times we had.'

In 1955 the room rental contract with the Primitive Chapel was finally cancelled after thirty-two years. There were plans to build a laboratory and a Housecraft Room on the school playground but neither materialised. However, in 1959, three new 'hut' classrooms (Rooms 17, 18 and 19) were provided to relieve the overcrowded main building, and Rooms 11 and 12 were converted into a Physics laboratory with a prep room. As a result of these changes, every classroom was given a new number. This caused much confusion to everyone at first but they gradually grew used to the more methodical arrangement. In the same year, Miss Swindells became Deputy Head.

*

Most Talked-About Staff

Miss Audrey Geraldine Garde de Courcey Smale BA, English & Librarian, 1954-76
She was born 3 Jan 1931, daughter of Captain Percy Walter De Courcey Smale, a prominent Wigan musician and organist at Wigan Parish Church, and Matilda of Orrell Hall. She studied English at Manchester. She was a poised and elegant lady who wore her academic gown with pearls. A talented and inspirational teacher and role model, she was always smiling, but disciplined in her approach, expecting and encouraging high standards. When LGGS closed she joined Leigh College. After retirement, she worked almost full-time in the Church of England as a Parish Administrator and Church Treasurer at Newchurch Parish Church. She died in 2009.

Mrs Harrison, Assistant Caretaker, 1921-53
The school magazine describes how, 'To many former members of staff and old girls she was a link with its continued progress. Changing conditions made the work of cleaning the school increasingly difficult, but she would not lower her standards, with the result that in spite of the dirt and pollution wafted in the building from pit and factory chimneys, the good order and cleanliness of the building was a pleasure to those who used it. Such service and loyalty from the individuals who worked together in the school

community – whatever task they were doing – enriched the whole life of the school.' She died in 1953.

Miss Olive Norminton BA, Geography, 1946-76

She did a wartime three-year degree course in two years at Manchester and celebrated her twenty-first after coming to LGGS. There was a rumour she had been engaged but her fiancé was killed in the war. She was considered a strict but excellent teacher who would take no nonsense from anyone. When LGGS closed she joined Leigh College. She retired in 1982 and died in 1988 at her home in Stockport.

Notable Events

In 1954 members of the school attended an illustrated lecture on 'The Ascent of Everest' by two members of the Everest team, G. Lowe and A. Gregory, at the Savoy Cinema, Atherton. A large party of girls was also taken to see the film *The Ascent of Everest* at the Regal Cinema, Leigh.

In March 1958, French assistant, Mlle Desvernes from Nancy University, tragically died after returning from Manchester with a school party. Disembarking from the coach, she looked the wrong way when crossing the road and was knocked down and killed.

In April 1958 there was a visit to the ITV studios in Manchester together with LGS to take part in the programme *Youth Wants To Know*. The panel was made up of two girls and four boys and the audience was comprised of Sixth-Formers from both schools. Vivien Eaves remembers, 'We were given tea in the modern canteen. Here we saw many odd-looking people being served; some obviously technicians, others with long curly beards and hair to match. Both panel and audience greatly enjoyed the experience of being on a TV programme and hearing the interesting views of the Roman Catholic bishop on present-day debatable points.'

The Old Girls' Association

The joint LGGS/LGS Dramatic Section, now known as 'The Grammarians', performed several one-act plays, and there were joint dances. However, there was some criticism that the band chosen by the Old Leighians didn't play the right music for dancing to. After several successful years, The Grammarians were disbanded and the money divided between the two associations. Table tennis was a popular activity along with netball (competing in the Manchester League), hockey and theatre trips. However, other activities failed to get off the ground and, although there were still over 200 girls 'in the book', poor attendance meant dances had to be cancelled to save losing money. In an attempt to persuade more Old Girls to join the Association, and particularly the committee, it was suggested that all school leavers be invited to attend two meetings before paying. The meetings were now held on the first Wednesday of Spring Term and the last Wednesday of Summer Term. There was a minor crisis as the minute book was lost.

Notable Alumni

Dr Eileen Read (née Hughes) (LGGS 1957-64), BSc Hons in Physics (King's College, London University). PhD in the field of Low-temperature Physics (Lancaster), awarded a Mullard Research Prize. Physicist at GEC Hirst Research Centre, Leader of the SAW and Quartz Crystal Group.

Image 27

Image 28

109

Image 29

Image 30

110

The 1960s

Image 31

Headmistresses: *Miss Hulme 1954-61 / Miss Swindells 1961-74*

Contributors to this chapter: *Gwen Kelleher (née Beaver, 1962-69), Pam Miller (née Johnson, 1962-67), Hazel Lyth (née Boydell, 1967-72), Carole Jay (née Marshall, 1965-72), Shelley Sephton (née Short, 1965-72), Aisla Wall (née Pearson, 1969-76), Kathleen Wood (née Ayre, 1959-64), Shirley Medling (née Pemberton, 1959-64), Alison Armfield*

111

(née Pownall, 1963-68), Doreen Hedley (née Hudson, 1966-68), Karen Thompson (née Marsh, 1969-76), Lynda Froud (née Boydell, 1967-74), Elizabeth Williams (staff, 1968-73)

*

In 1960 there was a reorganisation of all-age schools in the area which left Tyldesley Boys' County Secondary School empty. It was put to the LGGS governors that the school could transfer there but the motion was firmly rejected, the preference being for a new building next to the sports pitch at Pennington. Attempts were also made to move LGGS to a higher position in the Major Building Programme list but a new Leigh C of E School took priority. By the time Miss Hulme left in 1961, the original nine classrooms had increased to seventeen and the two laboratories to four, but there were over 600 girls and thirty-two members of staff. The Cookery classroom was too small to accommodate the regulation number of twenty-two and Music had to be taught in an ordinary form room or the Hall. Gwen remembers, 'One of the main features of the school as I moved through it was the lack of space. When I was a First-Former, we had assemblies in the Gym taken by Miss Smart, the Deputy Head, but on Fridays the whole school went into the Hall for assembly taken by Miss Swindells. We could just about fit in but, as the years went by, it became even more of a squash so whole school assemblies were only held at the end of term.'

Throughout the rest of this decade, Miss Swindells did her utmost to increase and improve the school's accommodation, constantly approaching the governors for their help. In 1961 an application for residential development next to the playing field reduced the amount of land available but in 1964 a plot near Marshall Street was

112

finally purchased for a new school building. Meanwhile, desperate to accommodate the growing number of pupils, the governors and Miss Swindells looked at buying 1 Gordon Street, but the terraced house was deemed too impractical. Instead, the LGGS building was rewired, repainted and a new central heating system installed along with a modern floor surface on the lower corridor. The stage in the Gym, a remainder from its early days as the Hall, was also removed to create more floor space. In 1966, Honiston Street was blocked off to traffic to create an extension to the playground at the adjoining Sacred Heart School. This had always been the main access route to LGGS so a new front access gate and driveway had to be created off Windermere Road, and a new rear gate entrance provided on the west side of the Kitchen/Dining Room.

Before the war there were less than thirty in the Sixth Form, but there were now approaching ninety so they had to use rooms in the Technical College and Leigh CE Junior School in Henrietta Street. As Gwen remembers, 'We certainly got plenty of fresh air walking to our lessons.' In addition to those moving up through the school, girls were allowed to transfer from secondary modern schools and other grammar schools. It was a source of pride to Miss Hulme that a larger Sixth Form meant 'more girls now undertake further professional training on leaving school to fit themselves for a more varied and interesting life'. But not all girls could afford to stay on, as Pam remembers, 'Miss Swindells didn't want me to leave straight after O-Levels but Dad wanted me to work in the shop.' Other girls, like Hazel, 'just wanted to be out in the world as a working person and a scientist, so I got a job at Sutcliffe Speakman, which you could do easily then.'

The girls had always been encouraged to consider different options after leaving school, and Miss Swindells introduced the first Careers Convention with each classroom acting as a consulting room for two experts. There were fifty-three in total including representatives of the Police Force, the Armed Services, and science- and arts-based employers. Teaching, of course, was always an option and many old girls went to university or teacher training college then returned to join the staff, among them Avis Freeman (née Grundy), Norma Dornan and Anne Thompson (née Parry). There was a particularly high turnover of staff during this period with new teachers replacing those who were moving on to different schools, taking a career break to start a family, or simply retiring like Miss Marlow who left in 1964 after thirty-six years at the school.

It was during this decade that some of the older staff started to find it harder to discipline, or even teach, the girls despite their many years of experience. There was a growing generation gap, and the younger staff, who had attended teacher training courses after or as part of their degrees, employed more modern and interactive teaching methods. When the school opened in 1921, most of the staff had only a degree in their chosen subject, but in 1964 82% were trained teachers. This prompted some criticism of 'untrained' traditional teachers like Miss Seacombe, as Carole remembers, 'She used to stand at the front of the room in her gown, gazing out at the Parish Church, reading from her own school history file and you just had to take notes.' Miss Seacombe wasn't the only teacher still employing this method and perhaps, after many years of delivering the same lessons, she found them as dull as some of her students did. Shelley remembers, 'She was sat at the front whilst we revised, but she was nodding off. Every time she nodded off one of us left the room so by the end there was nobody left.' But Aisla says, 'as a form teacher Miss Seacombe was good fun and used to tell us staffroom gossip.

114

At the end of the school year she invited us all to her house for an evening supper. About eighteen of us. It was exactly as we'd imagined: a big, dark, old-fashioned house, very gothic with loads of cats and cat ornaments. Even the toilet roll holder was a cat.'

Today, with so much technology available in schools, it is important to remember just how basic the teaching equipment was at this time and how much the teachers had to rely on their own ability to communicate and hold the attention of their class. Some used their knowledge and skills to impress. Carole remembers Miss Norminton who, 'could walk up to the blackboard and draw a fantastic map of Australia or North America from memory'. Some teachers were relentlessly positive and dynamic, like Mrs Owen who, Gwen recalls, 'Took me in hand in the third year. My worst subject was Maths but "Girls," she would say in her lilting Welsh accent, "Whatever job you get when you leave here, you will need Maths O-Level and I aim to make sure you get it."' Other teachers simply seemed to have a special indefinable aura. Take the universally admired, respected and much loved Miss Smale, who Kathleen describes as 'a fantastic English teacher and very elegant. She seemed to glide down the corridors like a majestic galleon in full sail. She instilled in me a lifelong love of the English language. To this day I can't bring myself to use the word *nice* as she said it was non-descriptive and showed a lack of imagination by the user.'

Despite the talents of such teachers, there was a perceptible shift in attitude and some girls started to rebel. They felt the influence of the 'swinging sixties' through music, fashion and TV programmes which opened up a wider world beyond their own quiet corner of East Lancashire. The decade was a time of changing attitudes, alternative lifestyles and the rise of a youth culture which challenged authority and its outdated conventions and restraints. Amongst these were the school rules, now seen by many to be too restrictive and even petty. Shirley remembers, 'Everyone was proud when I passed the 11+ but the uniform was very expensive. So my mum, who was a tailoress, made me the culottes to play hockey in. But they weren't the exact shade of navy blue and Miss Swindells sent me home. My mum marched me back in and said they were as good as anyone else's, if not better. Not long after I started at the school, my mum died. There was only me and my dad and I had to do the ironing. One day I went in a crumpled shirt and Miss Seddon said, "Why hasn't your mother ironed your shirt?" She was my form teacher. She should have known about my mum. But there was no bereavement counselling then.'

Other old girls remember being put in detention for wearing white knee socks instead of grey, having their hat brim turned up instead of down, or rolling their skirt up to create an improvised version of the fashionable 'mini'. The rule about not eating outside the school in uniform was still rigorously enforced but often disobeyed, usually when travelling to and from the sports pitch. Carole remembers, 'You were supposed to go via the Turnpike but we went down Cook Street because there was a shop down there that sold muffins.' The walk to the pitch remained as unpopular as ever, as Gwen recalls, 'I loved hockey but, my goodness, was there ever such a cold and windswept place?' Carole again, 'One girl had a disability so was allowed to go down to the pitch on her bike but she still had to take part when she got there.' Others used to deliberately take their time walking down so that the hockey team had been picked before they'd got changed. Some avoided hockey all together by hiding in the the *Wimpy Bar* on Market Street until they were discovered by an irate Miss Dornan.

Another unpopular rule was that girls must not leave the school at dinnertime without an official pass, even though, as Alison remembers, 'There was nothing to stop us going out. There was no monitoring of the coming and going, it was just a rule. You'd see the teachers in the Dining Hall but not in the playground. We were just expected to behave because we were ladies.' Nevertheless, the 'ladies' found ways around the rule by forging letters to say they were going home for lunch, then bunking off to the chippy or even climbing out of the form room window to go to the pie shop at the top of Windermere Road.

The frustration of some girls led to behaviour that was, at best, mischievous and, at worst, a health and safety risk. Alison remembers, 'At the front of the school was a little lawn that we weren't supposed to go on but we went round there with a Guide pen-knife. We took it in turns to throw the knife down between another person's legs. We never got caught – or injured anyone.' Shelley recalls Miss Crankshaw used to come into the classroom, lean on a chair and put her hand on the cupboard, 'so we moved the cupboard and she fell on the floor. We all shot up and ran to her aid, laughing. It was just harmless, childish, silly fun. We hid all the board rubbers once, threw them over the wall into the market skips, or put them on top of the board so when the teacher rolled it down they fell off.' It seems St Trinians had nothing on LGGS as other old girls remember sneaking under the stage and floorboards to smoke, climbing out of windows to run round the building, putting drinking straws inside the works of the Hall piano, or banging desk lids in unison. This may also have been the decade when the tradition arose of providing a guard of honour from the Dining Room for new girls on their first day. This was followed by tying them to the railings or netball posts with their girdles. Some old girls also remember having their tie flicked or even being hung by their collar on a coat hook in the Cloakroom.

Unfortunately, some girls took things a little too far. Doreen remembers transferring to LGGS in the middle of a crime wave, 'There was minor shoplifting going on at lunchtime with girls taking little things, like pencils, from *Woolworths*. They were caught that same day. Everybody was hauled before Miss Swindells and their parents were brought in.' Two girls also made the newspapers in December 1963 when they went to see the Beatles. Miss Swindells had refused to allow Gillian Brighton and Elaine Shoreman to queue for tickets at Liverpool's Empire Theatre but they decided to go on the day anyway. Elaine stayed at Gillian's the night before so they could catch a bus together to Liverpool in the morning. They went to George Harrison's home and his mother gave them tea before they went to the theatre. On hearing about their journey, the Beatles agreed to meet them. Despite their enthusiasm, however, the two girls said they would never scream at their idols, they preferred to listen. 'And,' said Elaine. 'I think they could do with a bit of a haircut.'

Perhaps it was this incident that made Miss Swindells decide to reintroduce the House system in 1964, providing extra guidance from the House Mistresses and some peer pressure. According to Gwen, 'We were all invited to think of suitable names for the Houses. John, Paul, George and Ringo were quite popular choices but local beauty spots won the day.' In fact, they were named after famous Lancashire Hills: Coniston, Longridge, Pendle and Rivington. On Thursdays, the House assemblies met in the Hall, Gym, Dining Room and Annexe Hall. Over the following years, each House competed to win several awards including the Challenge Shield, the Swimming Trophy, the Heyes House Trophy and the Work Trophy. Coniston, led by Mrs Taylor, ran green-themed stalls at the annual Autumn Fair, reached the final of both hockey and netball competitions and sold over a thousand LGGS-labelled ballpoint pens for charity. They were unsuccessful in the Music Festival but the House captain claimed 'this only goes to show that the other houses were brilliant because we were very good.' Longridge, led by Mrs Seddon, indulged their love of dramatics by creating living waxworks for the Autumn Fair, joined forces with Rivington for a talent contest and won the Work Trophy for two terms. According to their House captain they 'didn't do as well academically but made up for it with sport'. And they supported Lady Hoare's Thalidomide Appeal. Pendle, led by Miss Moore, formed a relationship with the National Children's Home at Frodsham, adopting a 'family group' which they treated to Easter eggs and a trip to Chester Zoo. As *Pendle Panthers* they beat *Rivington Rovers* in a mock football match, and finally won the much coveted Work Trophy. Rivington, led by Miss Lawrenson, organised a witch's cavern at the Autumn Fair where they sold minerals and played pop records. But representing the school at a stall at Leigh Infirmary's annual Garden Party did not make up for their many bad marks and detentions.

Girls were encouraged to work co-operatively in their forms. Gwen remembers, 'In the second year, our form room was the Art Room on the first floor. Each week we used to get points for tidiness and the form with the most points got the Tidiness Trophy at the end of term. We always used to reckon we had the hardest job with the Art Room because other classes used to leave a terrible mess when they had a lesson. We also used to get a trophy for flower arrangements. Each form would elect an artistically inclined girl who would collect a few pennies each week from the rest of us and buy flowers to put on the teacher's desk. Our flower girl was Barbara Bentley and a grand job she made of it year after year, winning the trophy for us several times.' Flower monitors were allowed to go and buy their flowers from Leigh Market which, in 1967, moved to a new building next door to the school.

Miss Swindells encouraged greater pride and respect for the school by reintroducing the whole-school photograph in 1962. Presumably this is also when the rumour started that you could appear on it twice if you ran round the back once the camera had started moving. In 1963 the Headmistress stressed the need for recreation and rest at weekends and during school holidays, arguing that part-time employment was proving a hindrance to the girls' studies. However, for many of them, this work provided the money needed for extra costs such as membership of the school's societies. Clearly the school was also looking for ways to cover its own costs, as in 1961 the school magazine featured its very first advertisement for *Danby's Outfitters*.

Music continued to be an important part of school life, and the once woeful orchestra was now much expanded and improved. It rehearsed and performed regularly. All of the school's musical groups gave concerts, played at school events and entered the Wigan Music Festival, winning several prizes. Perhaps this is why Karen was advised to 'put my recorder under my seat and play on a twelve inch ruler as I was putting everyone else off.' A new Art Club was formed to compliment the Craft Class which specialised in oddly shaped baskets but also acquired a kiln to make pots and ceramics. The Folk Dancing Society continued despite clashing with other societies and the Modern Languages Society introduced French folk dancing. The Classical Society diminished but the Literary Society flourished under the guidance of Miss Hughes, now assisted by Miss Smale and others. There was even a Junior Book Club with orange juice and biscuits. The Film Society came and went but was revived yet again by Miss Smart and members enjoyed watching *The Wizard of Oz* and *The Red Shoes*. A new Dramatic Society was formed and performed Henry Purcell's *Dido and Aeneas* opera for four nights, while the Junior Dramatic Society continued to thrive. Both groups performed in the school Hall, using the Biology lab as their green room, and appeared in the Leigh Drama Festival at St Joseph's Hall. Members of the Student Christian Movement, now the Christian Education Movement, enjoyed lectures illustrated by colour slides, and attended conferences on the Christian faith. Meanwhile, the Chemical Society, a relatively short-lived affair, demonstrated how to turn water into wine. The Scientific Society was accompanied by the Naturalist Society led by Mrs Freeman. They used Lilford Woods for fieldwork and arranged a Pets Show at the school with a wide range of entries from horses to hamsters. The popular Astronomy Class borrowed a Japanese planetarium so the girls and members of staff could see the simulated night sky suspended from a beam in the Physics lab.

The Library was transferred to the hut next to the main building in 1962 and a new automatic bell system installed across all the playground buildings. The Library was only open during the dinner hour, but was very popular, particularly after it was furnished with new chairs. It also doubled as a Sixth Form room, their lockers lining the walls outside. The Senior Debating Society continued as did the Sixth Form talks in Senior assembly, but a new Sixth Form Society was formed to provide both serious and light-hearted school activities for its members. One such activity was arranging an annual party in the school for children with a physical disability. A School Charity Committee was formed with a representative from each form and some staff members. From 1961 to 1967, this committee adopted the Polish-Ukrainian Juzicz family who had been displaced in

Germany. Money was raised to buy them essential furniture, food parcels and clothing, and nearly every girl in the school pledged to give a penny a week to charity. In 1966 thirty girls voluntarily undertook to visit and make friends with a number of elderly people in the vicinity of the school. The Fifth- and Sixth-Formers paid regular or weekly calls in pairs, which a commentator in the school magazine claimed was 'yet another indication that the school, in offering full education, is producing not simply "examination fodder" but girls who are interested in serving the community.'

Netball and hockey continued to be very popular along with tennis which was played on the sloping playground courts. A wire fence was later fitted around them as so many windows had been broken. There were advanced swimming classes with awards offered by the Royal Life Saving Society or the Swimming Teachers' Association. The Athletics Club met every Wednesday after school with extra training and coaching to improve performances. This resulted in some girls being chosen to represent Leigh in the Lancashire County Championships at Belle Vue. Lynda wasn't one of them, 'Mrs Thompson was at my auntie's funeral and Avis Freeman asked her if she remembered me, Lynda Boydell. She got all excited and said I was a brilliant sportsperson until I told her that two of us had the same name. I was the one who narrowly avoided impaling Mrs Turner with a javelin as my aim was so bad.' Some girls were chosen to represent the North West area, one attended the Women's Amateur Athletic Association, and Lesley Evans was chosen for Olympic 80m hurdles training at Lillieshall Hall in 1966.

There were lots of school trips and holidays with all transport arranged by the efficient School Secretary and Bursar, Miss Bent. These included day trips to plays, exhibitions and conferences in Manchester, Padgate and

122

Liverpool, plus one exotic trip to Povah's butchers in Leigh to see a demonstration of the carving of a cow. Longer trips ranged from a Mediterranean cruise to the Near East, when six Sixth-Formers joined 800 other schoolgirls from all over Britain for an educational cruise on the SS *Nevasa*, to hiking and youth-hostelling in Derbyshire. One hiker noted, 'We were soon able to tell we were back in Lancashire, because of all the chimneys in smoke.' The smoke, combined with damp winter air, created smog and the girls would long for it to obscure the church clock as that was the signal for them to be sent home early.

In 1968 all members of the Sixth Form were given prefect duties. Ten senior prefects were then elected to organise a team of her fellow prefects. The prefects wore red ties and the Seniors blue. 1969-70 was a particularly difficult year for the school. The British secondary school population had increased by 300,000 since 1960 creating a national shortage of teachers; teachers were striking for better pay, and Miss Swindells was off sick. Elizabeth Williams came to teach English at LGGS during this time, 'Beryl Smart was effectively running the school as Deputy Head. She was extremely efficient. I was only in my twenties but Miss Swindells seemed to me to be moving towards retirement. She was very amiable but the less you bothered her, the happier she was. Some of the staff members at LGGS were slightly eccentric. The English department was headed by Vera Hughes who liked things doing her way and could become quite emotional. She used to spend hours sticking text books back together with sellotape. She had a mission never to throw out a book no matter how damaged. It was a matter of principle. Others were great fun, like Margery Barnes, Barbara Moore and Eileen Edwards who came in once with her hair dyed green and said, "This should silence the Fourth Form".'

As the seventies approached, the girls were encouraged to keep up with changes in technology, science and the arts. The Principal of Leigh Technical College, Dr Owen, invited sixty-four Maths students to look around the Electronics Department. They tried their hand at assembling simple circuits for the first stages of constructing a computer which was later brought across to the school. The Astronomy students considered the problems of the Apollo Seven spacemen, and members of the English sets met novelist Julian Mitchell and playwright John McGrath as representatives of the Arts Council. The Sixth-Formers even attended lectures on how to drive and how to deal with a skidding car.

Gwen says, 'I thoroughly enjoyed my time at Leigh Girls' Grammar School (we used to lose a mark if we omitted the apostrophe at the top of an exam paper) and remember it with great affection.' Alison comments, 'When I was at school I didn't want to conform and struggled with my identity. But when I finally became a lecturer I realised that I'd done what they told me to do.' Doreen recalls, 'I became very political and I credited that to going to grammar school. I was taught there was nothing I couldn't do and I embraced that. It was a time of real change, of not being put in a box any longer, the forerunners of women rebelling and answering back. It empowered me as a woman.'

*

Most Talked-About Staff

Miss Norma Dornan PE Dip, PE, 1964-76
She was born 20 December 1932. Ex-LGGS (1944-51), she attended Matlock Training College. She taught PE, games, tennis, netball, swimming and hockey and, although strict,

was well respected and popular. When LGGS closed she joined Leigh College. Although she always appeared fit and healthy, she was a heavy smoker and sadly died aged only sixty in 1993 following heart bypass surgery.

Miss Nellie Marlow BA, French, 1928-64
She became Acting Headmistress during Miss Perrott's absence in 1937. Senior Mistress 1938-39, she became Head of Department in 1945 but after a period of ill health spent a year in Paris to recuperate and returned as Senior Mistress in 1948. She retired as Senior French Mistress in 1957 but continued to teach some forms. She had lots of personal contacts with France and French people which enabled her to give her pupils a real appreciation of the country.

Miss Vera R. Hughes MA, English, 1957-76
She was born 8 May 1917 and lived her early life in Birkenhead, studying English at Liverpool. Her nickname was 'Tilly' and she was always remembered for wearing floaty frocks, tweed skirt suits and beads. As Head of English she set high academic standards and inspired a love of the English language. She retired in 1976 and died on 1 January 2010.

Notable Events

In 1960 Mr Aspinall of Leigh Technical College presented the school with a beautifully carved oak stand made for the antique Bible box presented the previous year by Miss Bent.

In 1967 Mr Humphreys retired after being School Caretaker since April 1939.

In 1969 Miss Langford (ex-LGGS) left to take a new appointment after being School Meals Supervisor since 1949.

The Old Girls' Association / Leigh Girls' Grammar School Association

There was a discussion about renaming the organisation. Suggestions included The Former Pupils' Association, Former Girls' Association, Old Grammarians Association, Grammarians Association, The Grammarians, Former Students' Association, The OG Guild and The OG Association. Most members objected to the word 'old' being included so, after much debate, it was decided to adopt the title Leigh Girls' Grammar School Association. A new constitution was drawn up as no record could be found of any previous constitution. However, the original constitution was later discovered in the missing minutes book. It was decided to broaden the aims of the Association and raise money for charity. Numbers continued to fluctuate so it was difficult to plan pre-booked events such as theatre trips. Losses were also made on the Christmas Dance and film shows. However, new activities were more successful, including make-up and cookery demonstrations, coffee mornings and car treasure hunts, and the financial situation gradually improved. The annual dinner, held at *Waterfields* restaurant on Leigh Road, was very popular but a large number of old girls who attended were not members so the price of the meal had to be increased. *Armstrong's* restaurant on Bradshawgate was chosen for the last dinner of the decade. Some concern was expressed about the future of the school and how that might affect membership of the Association.

Notable Alumni

Lesley Richards (née Evans) (1949-2011). A successful schoolgirl athlete representing LGGS and Leigh Harriers, she won the 1963 Junior High Hurdles English Schools Championship, was Lancashire Schools Sprint Hurdles Champion in 1963, 1964 and 1965, and a junior international against Canada. She gave up her sport when her job as a journalist clashed with training nights. At one time she was the only female reporter in an office full of males. She worked for the *Leigh Reporter* 1966-70, became Sub-editor of the *Wigan Evening Post* and *Wigan Observer*, then Editor of the *St Helens Star* and the *Leigh Reporter*. She retired in 1996 but returned as a columnist for the *Leigh Journal* in 1998.

Image 32

Image 33

Image 34

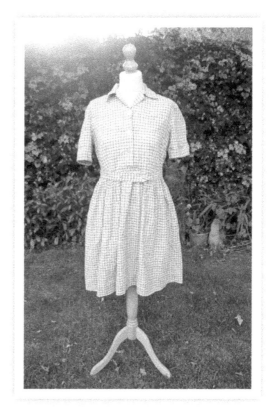

Image 35

The 1970s

Image 36

Headmistresses: *Miss Swindells 1961-74 / Miss Smart 1974-76*

Contributors to this chapter: *Carole Jay (née Marshall, 1965-72), Julie Woodward (1967-73), Alison Armfield (née Pownall, 1963-68), Dawn Halliwell (née Smith, 1975-80), Caroline Reid (1971-76), Hazel Lyth (née Boydell, 1967-72), Avis Freeman (née Grundy, 1949-56), Lynda Froud (née Boydell, 1967-74), Yvonne Parr (née Croston, 1972-76), Shelley Sephton (née Short, 1965-72), Christine Moss* *(née Matthews, 1972-77), Sue Hicks (née Fearick , 1974-79).*

*

The 1970s were turbulent years for the country with industrial action by miners, nurses, electricity workers, health workers and teachers, amongst others. In 1970 alone, over ten million working days were lost through strike action. LGGS was facing its own troubles with the looming threat of reorganisation into the comprehensive education system. The 1944 Education Act had led to a 'tripartite' system of grammar schools, technical schools and 'secondary modern' schools with local authorities responsible for their own secondary school provision. But there was a growing pressure for change, particularly from the Labour Party, and by 1963 over half of local authorities in England and Wales were working on comprehensive reorganisation. Wigan closed its grammar schools in 1972 but it took Leigh longer as they first had to provide a college to replace the two grammar school Sixth Forms. Ironically, this would be built on the land at Marshall Street originally bought for a new LGGS building. In the meantime, the former Ministry of Social Services office in Grasmere Street was leased to provide a much needed 'annexe' for LGGS.

The school celebrated its Golden Jubilee in 1971. A committee was formed by the staff with four aims: to hold the Prize Day in a hall where numbers could be unrestricted; to let parents and friends see the school at work; to give a commemorative gift to the town of Leigh; and to celebrate the fiftieth birthday on September 22 with a surprise programme for the girls. The first aim was achieved on the evening of Thursday 11 March with the Prize Day held in the grand and historic Free Trade Hall in Manchester. Over

1000 girls and guests were transported in a fleet of coaches and cars. The guest speaker was the Vice-Chancellor of Manchester University who stressed that 'there have never been so many or such varied openings for girls in further and higher education as there are at the present time'.

In April, two Open Days were held to give visitors a glimpse of the kind of work and activities which made up a normal school day. There were live performances of music and plays, gymnastic displays, cookery demonstrations, arts and crafts exhibitions, live science experiments and much more. In May the annual Commemoration Service was held at Leigh Parish Church with an address by the Bishop of Manchester, but the most important and memorable Jubilee event happened at the school on Wednesday 22 September. The girls were surprised to discover that, after morning break, lessons were to be abandoned for the rest of the day. Each form was taken in turn to the Cookery Room to see four enormous birthday cakes, each iced in a House colour and topped with a sugar plaque bearing the school's name, the dates 1921 to 1971 and the outline of a schoolgirl holding an open book. The cakes would later be cut into 700 pieces by the Upper Sixth, ready to be distributed at the end of the day. After break, the Seniors had a quiz while the Juniors went to the Staff Birthday Entertainment in the Hall. Solemnly, the orchestra took their places on the stage, dressed in LGGS uniform of various vintages, with Miss Swindells wearing a large Head Girl's badge. There followed a memorable rendition of Haydn's *The Toy Symphony* which featured Miss Crankshaw on triangle, Miss Dornan on drum and Mrs Jeanes, wearing a Leigh rugby scarf to celebrate their recent Challenge Cup victory, spinning a rattle. Miss Smart then gave a brief history of the school. This was followed by a hilarious performance of *The Stolen Prince* and a spirited rendition of *Birthday Serenade arranged for Varied! Ensemble* by Miss Woolley. The finale was a variation on the *Eton Boating Song* with a chorus of:

> *And we all go to Leigh Girls' Grammar*
> *Where everyone toes the line*
> *And there's nowhere like Leigh Girls' Grammar*
> *For having a jolly good time.*

The performance was repeated in the afternoon for the Seniors while the Juniors did the quiz, then at 3pm everyone went to their House meeting to collect their slice of cake. The commemorative gift to the town of Leigh was an elm tree which was planted in the Town Hall square in front of the new Library, accompanied by a second tree presented by the Leigh Girls' Grammar School Association. Carole has clearer memories of the huge cake than the staff show but vividly remembers an event earlier in the year, 'One girl refused to attend a gymnastics display because Leigh were in the semi-final of the Challenge Cup that day. As an essential member of the team, we finally managed to persuade her to take part but only on the understanding that a younger girl would come to the Gym door at half-time to reveal the result. So we were in the middle of the display when a little voice piped up from outside announcing the score.'

Miss Hughes wrote the editorial for the Jubilee magazine, but revealed many years later, 'One source of information was Dr Lunn's *History of Leigh*, and one day shortly afterwards a very irate Dr Lunn stormed into school at dinner hour, still in his shirt sleeves, no collar or tie, and decidedly unshaven. He was probably annoyed because we had done the history ourselves and hadn't called on him to do it. I put it to him that the work was, after all, only a schoolgirl effort, implying we were not challenging his authority. So he went off uttering darkly that once such things got into print they took root.'

In 1972 there was a fire at the school. Luckily, it was spotted by a man on his way to work at the adjacent fire station and only the cycle shed was seriously damaged. A short while later, the school was broken into: one of several acts of vandalism during this time. Then the miners' strike affected the coal supply and the girls had to be sent home early as there was no heating. In the same year, the school leaving age was raised to sixteen meaning more girls would gain O-Levels, though this wasn't necessarily a given, as Julie remembers, 'I was really good at English and very often came top in English Language but I failed the O-Level because I got carried away with questions instead of pacing and timing myself. I was nowhere near the end of the paper. There was no exam preparation and I couldn't work it out. I did loads and loads of revision but I didn't know how to do exams. Maybe some people are just naturally good at it but I wasn't.' Alison agrees, 'We revised by learning parrot fashion. No-one ever taught us revision techniques. When you got your results you got a percentage and your position in the class. They would just tell you in front of everyone even if you came bottom. There was no "you tried your best", they just read out your name and position, so you felt embarrassed for people.'

Preparation was key, as Dawn recalls, 'Dad didn't believe in homework, so it was hit and miss whether I got mine done. He said if I was clever enough, I would pass my exams without it.' She continues, 'Grammar school could be really tough for a girl like me. I often felt ashamed of my background. I grew up on a council estate, and there was never any money. Some girls made fun of someone in my class who couldn't go on a school trip to Belgium because her mum and dad had just bought a new boat. I was

135

horrified. Dad was out of work a lot so I got free school meals and free uniform. Those on free school meals had to stand in a different queue to those who paid for lunch. The uniform didn't always fit me but there was no choice. We were so poor, my shoes had cardboard in to keep the water out.' Caroline backs up this experience, 'I certainly felt disadvantaged in coming from a working class background. We had to wear a navy blue blazer which had to be bought, at great cost, from *Boardman's Outfitters* on Bradshawgate. Everyone was expected to wear a navy blue straw hat with a red ribbon round it. It was horrible and made you very conspicuous on the way home. First Years had to wear a navy pinafore dress, white shirt, navy and red tie, navy cardigan plus a navy and red sash which had to have the knot on the right-hand side. Once in the second year, the knot could be moved to the back. Then in the third year onwards, we had the "luxury" of being allowed to wear a navy blue knee-length skirt. But the worst part of the uniform was the thick cotton, navy blue knickers and white Aertex polo shirt we had to wear for gym class. It was so undignified.' Towards the end of LGGS the much hated knickers were finally covered with navy box-pleat culottes and, later, a short blue skirt on which girls proudly stitched their British Association of Gymnastics Awards (BAGA) badges.

Hazel remembers, 'We were allowed to cut the top off the tunic in the second year. Most girls also cut the bottom off to turn it into a mini skirt but, because mine was generous-sized and had been turned up several times, I let it down creating a midi skirt. Then I cut the raglan sleeves off my sweater and hemmed the edges to turn it into a tank top. When I went into school on Monday morning I wore both with patterned tights and brogue shoes. Everyone else was tottering about in platform shoes but I was asked to go and see Miss Swindells at lunchtime. After demanding I explain how I'd modified my outfit, she said that it was okay as long as I kept my blazer on – but the tights had to go.'

In 1973, after a lengthy period off sick, Miss Swindells herself decided to go. Deputy Head Miss Smart, who had been Acting Headmistress in her absence, became the last headmistress of LGGS. To say farewell to Miss Swindells, the staff devised another musical entertainment which included yet another version of the *Eton Boating Song*:

In 46 she came here
A maiden so young and fair
Of all that was to follow
She was probably unaware.
And we all go to Leigh Girls' Grammar...

Her retirement gift to the school was a collage and embroidery composition entitled *Trinity* which was hung near the main entrance in the bottom corridor. In return, the staff ordered a television for her from a shop in Wigan. Miss Smart and Miss Smale went to collect it. Avis continues the story, 'On arrival, Beryl said, "I'm Miss Smart. We're here to collect a television ordered for Miss Swindells." However, in their rush to set off, they had forgotten to collect the receipt and the salesman, already suspicious because of the surnames involved (he pronounced Swindells as *Swindles*), refused to hand the television over without it. Exasperated, Beryl told him to ring the school and speak to Miss Bent.' This convinced him he was dealing with swindlers and they both had to use their natural authority to make him hand over the television in time for the presentation dinner that night.

Miss Smart was a natural headmistress and, according to some of the staff, had effectively been running the school for a number of years as Miss Swindells eased into retirement. She was much more modern and progressive in her approach and had an ability to speak to people in a way that drew them in and made them interested. Lynda remembers, 'I ended up on the settle when I was late in from lunch after snogging my boyfriend by the school gate. Miss Seacombe had caught us and said, "Girl, what are you doing?" to which my boyfriend had replied, "What does it look like, you daft bat?" I was in floods of tears when Miss Seacombe went in to tell Miss Smart what had happened. But when I went in I could see she was trying not to laugh. She just handed me some tissues and told me to be more careful next time.'

Miss Smart was very good at sport and used to play hockey and tennis for the staff teams. She was also a talented actress and an inspirational Biology teacher who organised regular field trips to broaden the experience and interest of her students. Caroline says, 'At the time I didn't realise just how much the enthusiasm and competence of a teacher could influence your own interest and success in a subject along with your outlook and career choice.' Hazel remembers, 'I was a big reader as a child and loved *Mallory Towers* so LGGS was the nearest I could get to it. I really enjoyed the teachers being so different. They'd been educated far and wide, polymaths some of them. They would go off topic and tell you amazing things. Miss Crankshaw often went off into what would now be called Personal Social Education (PSE). "Right girls, I'll tell you some things you need to know in real life…"' Others, like Miss Hughes, were completely dedicated to their subject. Yvonne and Shelley remember, 'We invented all these rumours and fantasies about the teachers. We didn't really think about them having lives. But one summer we asked Miss Hughes if she was going on holiday and she said that she was going to the archives at Liverpool University to study.'

Carole recalls, 'Miss Dornan was my heroine and got me into teaching PE. I even went to the same college as her. She was very down-to-earth saying, "If you want to do this then this is what you need to do."' Miss Dornan, like most of the teachers, put a lot of time and effort into extra-curricular activities at the school. For many of them, it was an opportunity to explore modern culture outside the classroom. So while Miss Dornan taught ballroom dancing when the weather was too bad to send girls to the pitch, she also helped to choreograph dances for the new combined LGGS/LGS Sixth Form drama productions, written by LGS teacher, John Cassidy. Although the Folk Dance Group was still going strong, there were also Junior, Senior and Modern Dance Groups. Carole again, 'For *The Bull Leapers* production we choreographed a tumbling routine and then a dance to *Albatross* by Fleetwood Mac. We bought purple hot-pants to wear.' Yvonne and Shelley recall, 'Some joined the Drama Society just to mix with boys. We didn't see a boy properly until we were sixteen.'

There were other combined activities with LGS, including chess tournaments, hockey matches, an art and poetry anthology, *Six-Fifteen,* and even a debate on Women's Lib. Oh, to have been a fly on the wall at that event! LGGS girls had always been encouraged to formulate and voice their opinions and were now encouraged to do so in the Public Speaking and Debating Society, and the Fourth Form Monday Four Club. On the initiative of the Leigh Business and Professional Women's Guild, the school held an evening of Public Speaking and later took part in the National Public Speaking Competition in Preston. School teams also competed in a *Top of the Form* contest in Wigan.

Miss Smart encouraged extra-curricular activities saying, 'Academic achievement and training in student skills [...] are only one facet of education. All of our other activities also have a vital role to play in training the girls to participate in the life of a community, to work with other people in developing leisure interests which will continue with them into adult life.'

Music continued to grow from strength to strength under Miss Woolley with the orchestra and Junior and Senior choirs performing regularly at the Carol Service, Commemoration Service and Prize Day, and regular musical evenings and concerts. The school year wasn't complete without an opera which seemed to grow in size and scale every year despite the tiny Hall stage. *Iolanthe* by Gilbert and Sullivan was a particular success. Shelley remembers, 'I played a fairy. We had to run round the side of the stage then up the stairs to sing as the Chorus, but Pamela Bent fell on her way up and no-one could sing for laughing. Then, halfway through the show, all the fairies nipped to the chippy in their make-up. Miss Woolley went ballistic.' The school became a music centre for the Wigan Met Youth Orchestra. However, Caroline remembers, 'I was denied any opportunity to play a musical instrument as my working class parents could not afford to pay for the lessons which were classed as extras.' Yvonne adds, 'In my family we didn't have any money for hobbies like Girl Guides and things like that, but through the school I got involved in sport. I joined the hockey team and eventually became the contact for the games teacher to ring to say whether the game was on or not. Then I rang everyone else. It was lovely being on the coach with girls of all ages. It was a very social thing.'

The hockey teams continued to do well whilst the netball team finally entered the Leigh District Netball League. This meant matches were played regularly after school rather than at weekends, which was just as well as the PE staff complained that too many girls were dropping out of the teams due to their Saturday jobs. Netball and hockey developed the girls' physical skills and stamina but also their independence and a thick skin, as Christine remembers, 'If we were playing an away match, you had to catch a bus outside the Library and hope the rest of the team knew where to get off. The staff went by car but always trusted us to get there [under our own steam] except at weekends when we all went together by coach to play Bolton, Whalley Range, Rivington, etc. We were considered to be snobs by some local schools like the Council School. They hated us and used to spit at us, trip us up and knock our hats off in the playground. You just hoped you could play then get out alive.' During this time, a small patch of ground outside the school was used for the improvement of stick work and control of the ball, but many hockey matches were cancelled due to bad weather. Meanwhile, some netball matches had to be cancelled due to bus strikes but they did beat local teams from LGS (though a boys' school, they played LGGS at netball) and the Technical College. Christine again, 'We ran our own netball practice. We'd queue up at the Staffroom door for a ball and a set of bibs and do our own thing. Then, after Miss Dornan had had a couple of fags, she would come out and say, "Well done, girls!", collect the ball and go in.' Tennis was successful with the First Six going undefeated in their Saturday matches for one season, while the school's athletes competed at district and county levels. The Gymnastics and Swimming Clubs flourished, with the latter winning the Birtles Trophy for the fifth year in succession at the Tyldesley Swimming Club Gala.

Other activities included the Chess Club, formed in response to the new popularity of the game generated by

American Bobby Fischer. The Naturalist Club continued to be popular with many activities and outings. On one trip to Chorley, its members were thrilled to discover that the Nature Trail guide had been drawn by the school's own Mrs Hinde. Meanwhile, the Junior Group, inspired by the school's menagerie of guinea pigs, hamsters, fish, gerbils and stick insects, organised a lively pet show with small animals in the Hall and dogs – and a goat – outside in the playground. The Christian Education Movement Group flourished and members attended many conferences and talks about a wide range of topics from exorcism to drug addicts in Holland. The Astronomy Group measured the universe, considered the problem of weightlessness in space and visited the Planetarium in London. There were slightly less glamorous, but equally informative, trips by the Upper Sixth Needlework Group to Intex Yarns, Tillie and Henderson's factory, and Courtaulds Mill. These reveal the strength of manufacturing in Leigh at the time and the school's close links to local industries. Despite regular careers talks which included films such as *The Engineer is a Woman* and *Commercial Artist,* Caroline says, 'The careers advice was extremely basic and comprised of, "If you are *clever* do A-Levels, if not then do a secretarial course or go into the Civil Service".' Conversely, Julie adds, 'A group of us decided we would like to learn how to type so we got together and went and asked if there could be typing lessons and were told, "Young ladies at the Grammar School are never going to need to learn how to type".' Carole remembers, 'Careers advice was on a very personal level rather than a formal talk. We went through school knowing that we could have a life over and above getting married and having lots of children.'

Not all of the activities were directly related to subjects. The Pottery Club experimented with coil and slab ware then progressed on to making casserole dishes, whilst the Film Society watched modern comedy films such as *What's Up Doc?* and *Doctor in Distress*. The Theatre Workshop prepared the scenery and props for school productions, and there were lots of trips to see classic plays and the very modern and controversial *Godspell*. There were evening ice-skating trips to Altrincham Ice Rink, hiking holidays in the Lake District, and skiing trips to France, Bulgaria and Austria where one old girl remembers, 'We had our first glimpse of our bronze-skinned ski-instructors.'

Back home in Leigh, the Municipal Borough Council of Leigh was being absorbed into the new Wigan Metropolitan Borough Council as part of the local government reorganisation scheme in 1974. As a result, the school's governors who had previously served under the Lancashire Education Committee had to step down and were replaced with a new board. This was to be supported by the new Parent-Teacher Association (PTA) established by Miss Smart. During the next two years they organised regular discos, and attended talks about 'Problems of Adolescence' and the secondary education reorganisation with input from Mr Stanhope of Westleigh Secondary School and Dr Gardner from the new Leigh College. The PTA raised money for a tea trolley, two tennis umpire chairs, several musical instruments and a colour TV rental agreement for one year. At the 1974 Prize Day, Miss Smart expressed her sorrow that 'One hears mainly criticism of the young people of today but the majority of them are responsible, compassionate, unselfish and unstinting in the time and effort they give to those in need'. Charity work continued to be a strong focus of the school, particularly within the Oxfam Group and the House system.

Coniston's fundraising efforts, on behalf of the local hospital funds and the Red Cross, included a 'Way-out

Dress' competition, a 'Tramps' disco and a 'Top of the Pops' competition in which the entries ranged from Elvis to the prize-winning group, The Osmonds. Longridge arranged a 'Name the Puppies' competition, a Bonfire disco, beetle drives and an 'Ugliest Witch' competition. They also competed as the *Longridge Lions* football team. Rivington held an Easter Bonnet parade, a 'Hot-Pants' competition, a 'Groovy Guy' competition, a lunch-hour disco and a crisp-eating competition. Pendle raised money for a children's home in Frodsham through a Halloween disco, an 'Odd Couples' competition, a 'Mother and Child' contest, several successful tuck shops and by competing as the *Pendle Panthers* football team. Finally, after what they described as 'too many painful years of darkness with members of other Houses casting a cynical eye in their dejected direction', Pendle achieved top marks one term and won the 'Top House' contest.

The school took part in a new venture organised by the Manchester branch of the Variety Club of Great Britain in aid of underprivileged children in the area. Each school selected a representative to walk around Manchester City's Maine Road football ground for one hour. Over the next four years, LGGS raised more than £2000 and won the Variety Club Shield twice.

1975 was International Women's Year, the year of the Anti-Discrimination Bill and the Equal Pay Act. At the Prize Giving, held at the British Legion, Miss Smart said, 'This is our last year as Leigh Girls' Grammar School and [...] we can be justly proud of the role we have played, through my six predecessors and their staffs, in pioneering and developing the education of girls in this area of Lancashire. An education which only seventy years ago had to be fought for is now taken for granted, although I sometimes feel that we forget too easily the hard-fought battles of those early pioneers of girls' education [...]. There is still evidence of discrimination on grounds of sex, which is often not recognised as such. Often it takes the form of an unconscious prejudice: a girl's education and career are of secondary importance to those of her brother; girls are not encouraged to take what are considered to be boys' subjects.Legislation alone will not remove such prejudice.' With secondary reorganisation looming in Leigh, Atherton and Tyldesley, she added, 'We must make it a top priority to ensure that each individual child is given the best opportunity to develop his or her full potential – irrespective of whether boy or girl – and ensure that the best traditions of all our present schools are not lost but incorporated into the new system. There must be true equality of opportunity for all.'

LGGS was determined to go out on a high, and in 1976 the school was awarded first place in the adult section of the Leigh Drama Festival for *Not in the Guidebook,* a comedy produced by Doreen Johnson. It was the first time the school had won an award in the adult section since the first festival in 1933. The school also came second in the youth section with the play *The Rising Generation,* a satirical view on women ruling the world which won the William G. Woods Cup. *The Prince Who Was a Piper* was performed in Denton Drama Festival and won the Barbara Olsham Trophy for the best entry. Meanwhile, John Cassidy penned the poignant *Departures* as the final production for the joint LGGS/LGS Drama Group.

LGS was to merge with the neighbouring Manchester Road Secondary Modern School to create Bedford High School which would be spread across their adjoining sites on Manchester Road. But LGGS was to merge with the Council School, in nearby Coniston Street, and Westleigh Secondary School, in Westleigh Lane one and a half miles away, to

145

create Westleigh High School. The intention was to develop the Westleigh site to accommodate all the extra pupils but the alterations couldn't be completed in time for the merger so the new school was initially to be spread across the three sites. This meant the LGGS girls could at least stay on in their former building, but it was of little comfort to those in the Lower Sixth who had to transfer to the new college at Marshall Street for their final year. Some chose to leave instead: as one old girl says, 'I couldn't bear going to Leigh College after six wonderful happy years at LGGS.' It was particularly hard on those who had only recently joined the school. I attended Sacred Heart School next door, and it had always been my ambition to attend LGGS, so when I arrived in 1974 to hear the school would close in 1976 I was devastated. The only consolation was that, following the merger, we would be taught in a separate set or 'stream' and continue to follow the LGGS curriculum. So, for the next two years we absorbed what we could of LGGS' culture and traditions and clung to them until we left, proud to still call ourselves LGGS girls. We wore our blazers, gingham dresses and sports kits until we were bursting out of them and had to replace them with the Westleigh High School uniform. We even tried to save the old basket-weave LGGS chairs when they were to be replaced with modern plastic seats. We grieved that we would never have the opportunity to appear on the Honours Boards. It was a difficult time for the teachers, too. With Mr Stanhope appointed as Headmaster of the new Westleigh High School, many of the older LGGS teachers simply chose to retire whilst others, including Miss Smart, applied for jobs at Leigh College or elsewhere. A small number elected to stay on at the school and continued to teach the LGGS girls until we had all left, then they were fully integrated into the staff of Westleigh High School.

The new amalgamated comprehensive school finally moved onto the site in Westleigh, and Leigh Central Primary School moved into the LGGS building. Sadly, there came a time when the teachers decided that it, and the Edwardian Sacred Heart building next door, were no longer fit for purpose and a new joint building was planned for the site. Ironically, Sue remembers a phrase we were taught to help us remember the location of the fire exits in the LGGS building, '*We Hope Good Sense Prevails*' (*W*indermere Road entrance, *H*all, *G*ym, *S*cience Lab and *P*ractical Room). Unfortunately, despite a strong campaign to save it, good sense did not prevail in this case, and the LGGS building was sadly demolished in 2010.

On 14 May, at the last School Celebration Day, the Reverend G. W. Bonson said, 'There is I believe a real sense in which LGGS will live on. It must live on in our lives – because it has had its indelible effect upon us all.' That effect was reinforced by *Smart's Circus*, another classic staff entertainment, on the very last day of the school, 2 July 1976.

But I will let Lynda Lee Potter have the last word. She described LGGS as 'the escape route for ordinary children and the pathway to a new life.'

Most of us would agree with her.

*

Most Talked-About Staff

Miss Christine L. Crankshaw MA, Scripture & History, 1970-76

She studied History at Oxford. A real character, both wonderful and eccentric, she was considered to be a brilliant teacher who was strict but fair. She organised the school's successful contribution to the Variety Club of Great Britain's sponsored walk. When LGGS closed she became Housemistress of Prior's Field School in Surrey.

Mrs Angela Jeanes BSc/AKC, Maths, 1969-76
She studied Mathematics in London. Deputy Head from 1974, she was described as a tower of strength who carried out all her many duties in a characteristically calm, pleasant manner and with supreme efficiency. She was particularly skilled at sorting out the intricacies of the timetable and curriculum and organising PTA activities and always seemed to have tremendous reserves of energy and initiative. She was considered to be a very good Maths teacher who, although serious about her subject, always offered the support girls needed. When LGGS closed she left to take up a post as Deputy Head at a new comprehensive school in Bedfordshire.

Mrs Jackie Alderson (née Woolley) BEd/LRAM/ARCM, Music, 1966-76
She studied at Lancaster University and was respected as an inspirational teacher who guided and encouraged the girls in their musical abilities. Girls knew where they were with her and she always appreciated their efforts. She was very encouraging but firm when necessary. When LGGS closed she went to Leigh College then became Deputy Head at Fred Longworth and later at Canon Slade.

Notable Events

In January 1972, The BBC's Mr Scott and Mr Walker of the radio programme *Speak* came to observe their show being experienced by two Fourth Forms.

In March 1973 the staff performed *1066 and All That* for the school.
In January 1976 a school party attended a lecture by Chris Bonnington about the 1975 Everest Expedition.

Leigh Girls' Grammar School Association / Old Girls' Association

It was decided to keep the Leigh Girls' Grammar School Association name. The *Pack Horse* in Bolton was booked for the successful Golden Jubilee Year dinner. Lady Barker, Head Girl 1929-30, was guest speaker and first Head Girl, Alice Baron, replied to the toast. The Old Girls made suggestions for the Jubilee celebrations at school and donations were made to fund a tree for the newly organised town centre square adjacent to the new Library. The subscription was increased to twenty-five new pence (five shillings). When the School Secretary Miss Bent retired, she was given life membership of the Association. The annual dinner moved between the *Pack Horse* at Bolton and the Formby Hall in Atherton because of the large numbers attending. There was concern about a lack of information on the proposed education reorganisation in the Leigh area. There was a presentation at the Darby Room for Miss Swindells' retirement but, by then, the Association's current account was virtually empty and no further life memberships could be considered due to the uncertain future of the organisation. The last school magazine was sent out to members and Miss Smart called an extraordinary meeting. Because of the reorganisation, the OGA would no longer be able to meet in the LGGS building, so it was proposed by Miss Bannister 'that the OGA in its present form should be terminated at the end of this academic year'. A large majority was in favour of continuing to have the dinner, so the remaining funds were used to give awards or prizes at the discretion of Miss Smart, and a new group was formed to plan the next dinner. An advertisement was put in the new *Leigh Weekly News*.

Notable Alumni

Tracie Bennett (LGGS 1972-79). Actor, singer and musician. Her many TV performances include playing Sharon Gaskell in *Coronation Street*. She has appeared in several films and over thirty-five stage productions, including playing Judy Garland in *End of the Rainbow* for which she won a Broadway World Los Angeles Award for Best Actress in a Play (Touring Production).

Image 37

Image 38

Image 39

LEIGH GIRLS' GRAMMAR SCHOOL.

TIME TABLE

Autumn Term, 19__.

Monday	Tuesday	Wednesday	Thursday	Friday
Biology	History	English R1	Maths	German
Geography	German	French	Mrs. Davi.	French
	R.E.	R.E. Turner	Biology	Maths
Maths	R.E.	German	R.E.	Games
French	English	miss Boydell	History	German
English	Maths	Geography	miss Seacombe	English
Biology 30	R.E. 30	PREPARATION German 20	Maths 30	German 30
French 30	German 30	English 30	Scripture 30	English 30
Geography 40	Maths 30	French 20	Biology 40	Maths 30
English 20	History 40	Geography 40	History 60	French 30

Image 40

Acknowledgements

Many thanks to all the old girls who shared their memories via letters, phone calls, interviews, emails and social media. Any memories of teachers are from a schoolgirl perspective and are not intended to be a general criticism of any individual or their teaching skills.

Particular thanks to Vivien J. Davies, Sue Kennerley and Linda Logan for posting and scanning missing LGGS magazines. Most of the additional information in the book comes from the LGGS School Magazines (1926-76), Borough of Leigh Council Minutes and the Minutes of the Governors of LGGS. Additional sources and detailed references can be found in a copy of this book supplied to Archives: Wigan & Leigh.

Grateful thanks to the wonderful staff at Archives: Wigan & Leigh for digging out boxes of minutes and listening patiently when I shared my finds with you.

Thanks to all the staff and my lovely friends at LGGS who made my school years so memorable and enjoyable.

Thank-you to Julian Watts (https://www.joolzdesign.com) for the lovely cover design and to CJ Harter (https://www.cjharterbooks.co.uk/editingproofreading.html) for careful copyediting and proofreading and seeing the book through the production process.

The biggest thanks go to my ever-supportive partner, Michael, for patiently putting up with yet another project, and to my loving parents for making it possible for my brother and I to both go to grammar schools.

Lightning Source UK Ltd.
Milton Keynes UK
UKHW011300120921
390444UK00002B/45

9 781803 021317